FAMILY PRACTICES IN LATER LIFE

Pat Chambers, Graham Allan, Chris Phillipson and Mo Ray

This edition published in Great Britain in 2009 by

The Policy Press
University of Bristol
Fourth Floor
Beacon House
Queen's Road
Bristol BS8 1QU
UK

Tel +44 (0)117 331 4054
Fax +44 (0)117 331 4093
e-mail tpp-info@bristol.ac.uk
www.policypress.co.uk

North American office:
The Policy Press
c/o International Specialized Books Services (ISBS)
920 NE 58th Avenue, Suite 300
Portland, OR 97213-3786, USA
Tel +1 503 287 3093
Fax +1 503 280 8832
e-mail info@isbs.com

© The Policy Press

British Library Cataloguing in Publication Data
A catalogue record for this book is available from the British Library.

Library of Congress Cataloging-in-Publication Data
A catalog record for this book has been requested.

ISBN 978 1 84742 052 7 paperback
ISBN 978 1 84742 053 4 hardcover

Cover design by The Policy Press
Front cover: image kindly supplied by www.alamy.com
Printed and bound in Great Britain by TJ International

For Anne Martin–Matthews

Contents

Foreword

Judith Phillips

The study of ageing is continuing to increase rapidly across multiple disciplines. Consequently students, academics, professionals and policy makers need texts on the latest research, theory, policy and practice developments in the field. With new areas of interest in mid- and later life opening up, the series bridges the gaps in the literature as well as providing cutting-edge debate on new and traditional areas of ageing within a lifecourse perspective. Taking this approach, the series addresses 'ageing' (rather than gerontology or 'old age') providing coverage of mid- as well as later life; it promotes a critical perspective and focuses on the social rather than the medical aspects of ageing.

One of the traditional areas of study within gerontology has focused on 'the family'. In this book Pat Chambers and her colleagues provide a critical analysis of the diverse experiences of family life for older people highlighting family practices and relationships. Different social, class, gender and ethnic-based relationships are discussed, as well as particular family relationships such as long-lasting relationships, older sibling relationships, grandparenting and the experience of later-life widowhood. Themes of continuity and change, flexibility, negotiation and complexity flow through the book reflecting the diverse and global nature of the family and providing clues as to the family's endurance across generations and history. The book provides a rich sources of literature on the family lives of older people and is valuable for both undergraduate and postgraduate courses in ageing, social policy, sociology, social work and health.

Preface

This book was conceived walking towards the Rose Gardens at the University of British Columbia, overlooking the Pacific Ocean. Pat Chambers was visiting UBC to talk with Anne Martin-Matthews and other colleagues in the School of Social Work and Family Studies there. Pat knew Anne through their shared interests in social gerontology; indeed, some years earlier Anne had been the external examiner on Pat's PhD. Graham Allan was in the middle of a two-year visiting fellowship in the School of Social Work and Family Studies at UBC. He had been seconded from Keele to the Family Studies Group at UBC as a result of Anne Martin-Matthews' appointment to research director of the Canadian Institutes of Health Research.

Pat had undertaken a small-scale research project on the part that siblings play in later life and, in addition to highly emotive discussions about the achievements and progress of Liverpool Football Club over the previous season, she and Graham spent some time talking how that research might be developed further. That afternoon, walking in the sunshine towards the Rose Gardens at UBC, they came to the conclusion that a book on the organisation of different family relationships in later life would be an interesting project, especially a book that focused less on the pathology of old age and more on the ways these relationships are managed in general.

From these beginnings the current book gradually emerged. Pat and Graham floated the idea with Chris Phillipson and Mo Ray, colleagues at Keele with strong gerontological interests. Both proved highly receptive to the possibility and 'signed up' to it. We approached The Policy Press and Judith Phillips, who at the time were in the process of launching their 'Ageing and the Lifecourse' series. We are very grateful for the support Emily Watt has given us throughout the process. Without that help the book may well have just remained only an interesting idea.

As it turned out, her support led to innumerable breakfasts among the four of us discussing the organisation of the book, the different chapters we might include and who would take responsibility for what. The typescript was eventually completed, a little more slowly than we had hoped. We would probably all admit that there were times when writing a book with three other authors seemed unnecessarily onerous, far harder than writing a single-authored volume. But none of us really felt this way for long. The four of us have worked very well together, proving supportive and positive, even when being critical.

In addition to Emily, we would like to thank our colleagues at Keele University. Collectively they provide a highly supportive academic environment that we much appreciate. We would also like to thank those who love us, not least our partners. They have come to accept our need to work at unreasonable times without losing the ability to remind us that there are more important things in life than getting a paragraph, section or chapter finished. Graham would also like to express his thanks to the School of Social Work and Family Studies – as was – at UBC for providing him with two terrific years. It was a privilege to be a member of the school. This brings us back to Anne Martin-Matthews. Although she probably does not realise it, without her influence this book may well never have been written. It is consequently to her that we dedicate the book.

Pat Chambers
Graham Allan
Chris Phillipson
Mo Ray
April 2009

Introduction

There is considerable public and political interest, particularly in the Western world, in older people and their families. Indeed, in line with what Means (2007) refers to as the 're-medicalisation' of old age at the beginning of the 21st century, a substantial body of literature has debated the role, responsibility and social policy mandate of the family in caring for an ageing population. Increasingly, what has been portrayed in these debates is what might usefully be described as a 'welfare model' of older families, in which family relationships in later life are reduced to: 'who cares for whom and in what circumstances?'. What has been missing from some of these debates, however, is a critical analysis that seeks to understand the experience and diversity of living in older families better. There is often little recognition, for example, that older families have a history of 'being', 'living' and 'ageing' together with scant attention paid to the multiple roles and complex relationships played out within those families. This is despite the wealth of evidence that most older people are enmeshed in a variety of often complicated inter- and intra-generational family ties.

Let us consider briefly the factual basis of this last statement. Data from the 2001 Census indicates that in England in 2001 the overall proportion of people aged 50 and over with living children was 86% for men and 88% for women (www.ons.gov.uk/census/get-data/index.html). Information on contacts with children is sparse, but recent data from the English Longitudinal Study on Ageing (www.ifs.org.uk/elsa) suggests that contact between generations is high, with the arrival of grandchildren leading to even more contact with adult children. Four-generational families are now more common, with one in four grandparents having a living parent. Furthermore, as a result of increasing rates of both divorce[1] and remarriage[2] or cohabitation, the number of older people on their second or third relationship is likely to grow. One consequence of this is an increase in stepchildren (and step-grandchildren). Increasing mobility, including living in different continents, means that while some families maintain contact at a distance through the use of old and new technologies others may have little or no contact.[3] Despite these considerable variations, a recent report from the Cabinet Office (2008) has identified that the family remains an important source of fulfilment, with the majority of people making considerable efforts to spend time with family. While there is clear evidence that relationship types are more fluid and that family composition now changes more frequently over the lifecourse, there is little evidence to suggest that increasing pluralism affects family relationships more or less negatively.

In this book we seek to make a contribution towards redressing what we perceive as an unbalanced and somewhat restricted portrayal of the family in later life. Rather than perpetuate a 'welfare model' of older families, our aim is instead to evaluate critically the diverse lived experience of family life for older people and how family life is carried out. By using theoretical frameworks drawn from sociology and critical social gerontology we seek to examine the complexity of that experience, the meanings attached to different family relationships and the way in which changing roles, structures and different ways of 'doing family' (family practices) impact on the lives of older people and family members.

A word on the methodology we have employed within this book: of necessity, given the paucity of research into family practices in later life, we have employed an eclectic approach that draws heavily on a broad range of available literature and research. Inevitably, this has been drawn largely from North America and Europe. Despite this limitation, we have tried wherever possible to address cross-cultural issues within individual chapters. We were very aware when undertaking this project that the voices of older people themselves are sorely lacking in relation to the 'ordinary' daily business of family practices in later life and we have sought to remedy that. In some chapters, we have used our own analysis of conversations with older people about family life to lead our discussion. In other chapters, where such analysis has been lacking, we have drawn on the voices of older people from the research of others to illustrate our discussion; we have not on the whole, however, sought to undertake secondary analysis. We feel justified in such an approach, given that research that explores the subjective experience and routine interactions of families as they grow older is still regrettably scarce.

It is now commonplace to locate one's own experience of family when 'writing about' the family (Connidis, 2001: xii). We are all over 50 years old – although it could be argued that we belong to different cohorts – and we are all members of 'older families', enmeshed in our own family roles, relationships and practices. Between us we comprise adult children, siblings, 'in-laws', parents and grandparents, step-parents and step-grandparents, partners ('long-term' and 'new'), aunts, uncles, nieces, nephews, cousins and so on. Those of us who are 'only children' also have people in our lives whom we regard as being 'like family'. We each acknowledge that our own individual experience of family life will inevitably influence to some extent our perspectives of the family in later life. Collectively, however, our experience of family life is extremely diverse, rooted as it is in different individual, family and socially structured biographies. A collaborative approach to writing this text has ensured that no individual, personal perspective is dominant.

In addition, in our professional lives we have a variety of research interests within critical social gerontology, sociology, social policy and social work, and we have separately researched and written about specific aspects of the family in later life. In that respect this book is a somewhat different venture, and is a collaborative, multiple-authored text that uses data collected from our own empirical and theoretical work as well as that of others. Naturally the content of the book reflects, to some degree, our collective, personal and research interests but we have tried to embed in the structure of the book a balance between theoretical considerations, *key* family relationships and what we perceive to be major issues in family practices in later life. Each chapter has a different focus but we have ensured that key themes – ageing, lifecourse continuities and discontinuities, experience, multiple relationships and roles, diversity, family practices and critical perspectives – are addressed within and across chapters.

Overview

We now provide an overview of what is to follow.

Chapter One, 'Family practices and family relationships', puts the experiences of older people in the context of recent theorising about the nature of family life. As well as focusing on different approaches to intergenerational relationships and the lifecourse, we explore how family relationships are actively constructed and patterned in later life. In particular, we examine how the concept of 'family practices' can be used to improve understanding of the family ties that older people negotiate.

Chapter Two, 'Families in later life', examines changing relationships and practices experienced by older people in the later stage of the lifecourse. Historically, the family has been viewed as a central source of support for older people, notably in periods of ill-health and dependency. We argue that intergenerational ties have been shown to be more complex than previously understood, with transfers of different kinds of support flowing downwards as well as upwards. A key observation is that it is probably now more helpful to think of different types of family life in old age, reflecting different social, biographical, class, gender and ethnic-based relationships.

Chapter Three, 'Older parents and their adult children', explores the complex and diverse relationships between older people and their adult children (who may themselves be parents and grandparents). Underpinning this chapter is the assumption that those relationships are situated within an individual and collective biography and that continuities and discontinuities over the lifecourse will affect the negotiation of family relationships, the meanings attached to those relationships, and family practices.

Chapter Four, 'Long-lasting relationships', signals the important role that is played by continuous long-term partnerships. Despite its importance as an established, sustained and central relationship, long-term marriage and non-heterosexual long-lasting partnerships remain an under-researched area. The paucity of research in this area is highlighted against the value of long-lasting relationships in the lives of older men and women. Drawing on empirical research with long-married couples, this chapter explores the ways in which older people define and construct their relationships.

Chapter Five, 'Brothers and sisters', highlights the contrast between the lack of interest in sibling relationships in later life in both sociology and gerontology and the way in which siblings feature in older people's own stories of ageing. Drawing on recent biographical research, this chapter explores the way in which older siblings negotiate continuities – and manage the discontinuities – brought about by ageing. A lifecourse perspective, grounded in critical gerontology, is employed in which individual and family biography, ageing, experience and identity are paramount.

Chapter Six, 'Grandparenting', is concerned with the ways in which older people 'do' their grandparenting. The main focus is on the character of relationships that grandmothers and grandfathers sustain with their grandchildren and the factors that shape this. It focuses on diversities in grandparental relationships as well as commonalties. In the light of recent shifts in patterns of partnership and marriage, it also examines the patterns of step-grandparent ties and contrasts these relationships with those sustained by 'biological' grandparents.

Chapter Seven, 'Later life widow(er)hood', focuses on the way in which older widows and widowers interact with family and/or wider kinship networks, and the extent to which cohort, gender and biography shape engagement in family practices and relationships. Drawing on a number of empirical studies, the chapter explores the complexity of roles and relationships that are played out. Living apart together (LAT) relationships are also considered within this chapter.

Chapter Eight, 'Globalisation and transnational communities: implications for family life in old age', examines the important development, associated with globalisation, of transnational families. The main argument developed in this chapter is that the phenomenon of globalisation raises important new concerns for understanding family life in old age. In general, the focus on globalisation confirms the importance of positioning individuals within the orbit of social and economic structures that are increasingly subject to forces lying beyond the boundaries of the nation state.

Our final chapter, Chapter Nine, 'Changing times: older people and family ties', considers the extent to which the family experiences of older people are likely to change over the next 30 years. We argue that as the lifecourse – in terms of both its family and non-family aspects – becomes somewhat less certain and more varied, so too the family relationships within individuals' personal networks are liable to be more diverse and more open to change. To illustrate this, and to reflect the themes of continuity and change presented throughout this text, we present a brief cameo from a study of stepfamily kinship that one of us was involved in. We conclude by reiterating the importance of a lifecourse perspective for understanding family life.

Notes

[1] For example, the proportion of divorced people aged 50–59 grew from 1% for men in 1971 to 12% in 2001; for women the increase was from 2% to 14% (ONS, 2001).

[2] In 2001, 16% of men over 50 had remarried and 14% of women (ONS, 2001).

[3] A survey in Great Britain in 2007 found that 44% of people over 70 had no close relative living nearby (Coulthard and Walker, 2002, cited in Department for Work and Pensions, 2005).

ONE

Family practices and family relationships

Introduction

There have been many changes in the patterning of family relationships over the last 40 years. While mid-20th-century family organisation was less uniform than the Parsonian emphasis on a conjugal/nuclear family system indicated (Parsons, 1959), the level of diversity now found, and accepted as normal, in people's experiences of family relationships is far greater than it was. In particular, since the 1970s, patterns of family and household formation and dissolution have altered quite dramatically and in ways that were certainly not predicted then. As is now widely recognised, the very idea of a stable, highly structured family cycle is no longer viable as an organising framework for understanding the dynamics of people's family life. Instead, the much looser, less deterministic notion of family course has become a more appropriate one for exploring people's family transitions. The central idea of the family course is not that people's family changes are entirely unstructured or haphazard, but rather that under contemporary social conditions the transitions that mark family life are inherently more fluid and thus less predictable.

There is a general tendency to assume that these changes have had a particularly marked impact on younger cohorts. Most certainly the family experiences of people currently in their 20s and 30s are quite different from those of people who are, say, aged 60 or over. Not only has the younger cohort been more likely to experience parental divorce and stepfamily involvement, but equally their typical partnership and childbearing trajectories have been quite different. The older cohort tended to marry early and have children at a relatively young age. In contrast, the younger cohort experienced greater sexual freedom, tended to marry later, frequently after one or more cohabiting relationships, and usually had children in their late 20s or early 30s. As importantly, there is now greater diversity – less uniformity around the mean, that is – in these patterns than there was previously.

It is important to realise that the changes there have been have also had direct and indirect consequences for the family relationships of older people. At some stage during their lives, they too may have experienced divorce, cohabitation with one or more others, remarriage and stepfamily relationships. As important, but less directly, they will have experience of their children (and grandchildren) following the more diverse patterns of family formation and dissolution now more common. In this regard, the historic family changes associated with late modernity – what Giddens (1992) refers to as the 'transformation of intimacy' – are generally having an effect on everyone's experiences of family life, old as well as young. In addition, of course, older cohorts' family circumstances also change as a direct consequence of ageing. Their children leave home, form new partnerships and have their own children. Their own parents die, perhaps after a period of infirmity. Their domestic circumstances alter further with retirement and changed lifestyles.

As this indicates, there are different levels of change influencing the process and structure of older people's family and household relationships. Following Hareven (1982), we can identify three distinct levels of relevance here. First, there are the types of historic change referred to above: social, political and economic transformations that have a continuing impact across a period of time. Second, there are cohort changes: changes that affect a particular cohort or age group because of the specific circumstances that have shaped their collective experiences. And third, there are age-related changes: changes that are consequent upon the lifecourse position of those in the cohort at a given age. It is the first and third of these that will be the prime concern of this chapter, and indeed this book.

There is one further distinction to clarify here, that between 'cohort' and 'generation'. Throughout the book we will be using the term 'cohort' to refer to a group of people who were born at a similar time and are consequently in a similar age group. In contrast, we will use the term 'generation' to refer to family relationships. Thus in this usage the first generation refers to the parents of the second generation, who are themselves the parents of the third generation, and so on. Similarly the first generation represents those who are grandparents to the third generation. As will become clear below, this distinction is important in order to avoid confusion between those times when our concern will be with experiences resulting from being part of a particular age group, and those when the concern is more specifically about the relationships between those occupying different positions in the family or kinship system.

The aim of this chapter is to consider the character of the changes that have been taking place in family life and to explore some of the different approaches that have been developed to understand them. As implied above, its principal focus will be on the increasing diversity that there is in people's family experiences. More specifically, it seeks to provide an analytical framework that helps place older people's contemporary family relationships in a broader context. However, the chapter will not be explicitly concerned with specifying in detail the content of recent changes in older people's family ties. This is the task of later chapters. However, in order to situate the different themes that this chapter addresses, it is necessary to consider in a little more detail the greater diversity that now characterises family life.

Diversity

The major demographic changes that there have been in family and household constitution are now widely recognised. Since the mid-1970s many western countries, including the UK, have witnessed: increasing numbers of people cohabiting, average age at first marriage rising, fewer people getting married and higher proportions of births to unmarried women (ONS, 2006; 2007). Similarly, there have been increases in the divorce rate during this time, in the number of second marriages, in the number of openly gay and lesbian unions and in the proportion of people living in single-person households (Allan et al, 2003). And while these changes indicate a higher degree of diversity in the ways people organise their domestic, sexual and familial lives, such diversity is compounded by the varied sequencing of these different domestic phases. As noted above, there is no longer the same strong ordering of the lifecourse that there used to be.

The social endorsement of this increased diversity in family patterns can be related to changing ideas of citizenship rights, the growth of individualism and a loosening of social controls over sexual behaviour. Indeed, the changes there have been generally demonstrate a reduction in the level of normative sanctions operating in the sphere of family relationships. To put this another way, the familial realm has become increasingly private. Family organisation is now seen less as a matter for public scrutiny than it was and more as a set of relationships and practices that, within certain legal bounds, individuals have the right to determine. In this regard, it is understood to be an aspect of private life over which others have comparatively limited rights to intervene unless someone is being harmed. The right of individuals to make their own choices about how they want their familial and sexual relationships to be organised is widely recognised. Even though others may disagree with these choices, they now have less legitimacy if they try to impose their own different values and beliefs on others.

The relative decline of normative sanctions concerning the morality of different ways of organising sexual partnerships and familial relations can also be recognised as representing a shift between structure and agency in family matters. It would be wrong to over-emphasise this; at one level new patterns of family organisation and structure have merely replaced older ones. However, as discussed, these new patterns do embody greater diversity in family structure and increased individual freedom and flexibility. Within the construction of our familial and domestic lives, we now exercise greater agency over the patterns of commitment and solidarity that we develop. This applies most obviously in our domestic and sexual partnerships, where the emergent de-institutionalisation of marriage has had a profound impact (Cherlin, 2004). But it also applies to other family and kin relationships, which are also now characterised by greater individual freedom.

Theoretical perspectives

The increased freedom we have over the patterning of our familial relationships has been reflected in recent sociological approaches to understanding family life. In the mid-20th century, functionalism – inspired particularly by Parsons (1959; Parsons and Bales, 1955) – provided the dominant sociological perspective for analysing family organisation. Although this approach has been heavily criticised over the years, not least for its apparent acceptance of a highly gendered division of work and employment, it still served as the theoretical blueprint for most family sociology. Certainly its emphasis on the normative construction of family relationships, albeit shaped by the relationship between family form and external structures, particularly the economy, dominated conventional understandings of why family relationships took the form they did. In essence the model assumed that, through their socialisation, individuals acquired relevant knowledge of how family relationships should be patterned and then somewhat uncritically applied this to their own behaviour. In turn, of course, such internalised norms were reinforced by the recognition that others also subscribed to similar beliefs about the ways that family relationships should be framed.

Negotiation

By the late 20th century alternative perspectives were developing that gave greater weight to the role of agency in the construction of family relationships and practices, in line with the greater empirical diversity evident in family life. One of the most important studies in this regard was Finch and Mason's *Negotiating family responsibilities* (1993), in which the authors examined the different relationships that adult children had with their ageing parents and the different responsibilities for providing support they felt. In this work, Finch and Mason posited that interactions in family relationships, and thus the family relationships themselves, are not constructed through people uncritically following conventional cultural rules or expectations. Instead, they argued that family relationships were generated through interactive processes that, while normatively informed, required the continuing agency of those who were, directly or indirectly, party to them. Relationships were built up over time through a series of interactions that were, in effect, negotiated in the context of the family environment in which they occurred (see also Finch, 2007).

There are three elements to this that warrant emphasising. First, Finch and Mason (1993) stress the need to analyse family relationships in context. While people's understandings of family morality and obligation are important in framing the ways they behave, so too are the circumstances of the individuals involved and the actions of the others within the pertinent family and kinship network. Individuals do not, in other words, simply follow a socially prescribed or given family script. Rather they are active in writing this script, doing so on the basis of their knowledge and experience of the different family relationships in question.

Finch and Mason's use of the concept of 'negotiation' serves to emphasise this emergent agential dimension of family relationships.

Second, Finch and Mason's (1993) conception of negotiation as a routine aspect of family relationships emphasises the importance of process in these ties. In other words, family relationships carry with them a history that shapes current (and future) interactions. Rather than being understood as a series of responses to particular contingencies and events, Finch and Mason's model highlights the emergent quality of relationships based upon people's experiences of previous interactions. Moreover this applies to the various relationships within the family network. Because of the interlocking character of family ties, knowledge of how different family members behave and respond across relationships, and over time, is shared. Importantly, as a result, individuals acquire reputations and 'moral identities' within their families that frame what others expect of them and form a backdrop to future interactions and negotiations between family members.

The third element of Finch and Mason's (1993) approach to highlight here concerns their use of the concept of 'negotiation'. As discussed above, they draw on this term to emphasise the active involvement of people in the construction of their family relationships. However, in using it they are not suggesting that family members routinely engage in organised negotiations of the form that typifies negotiations in the public sphere. Only rarely do family members sit down together with an agenda to sort out particular issues in the way that, say, employers and union officials negotiating employment conditions do. A far wider range of negotiation strategies are used in different families, and by different family members, in managing their relationships. Some of the negotiations that Finch and Mason (1993) are concerned with are explicit; some are implicit. Many combine implicit and explicit elements together in different ways. They specify three broad modes of negotiation that occur: open discussions, clear intentions and non-decisions. However, they emphasise that these should not be seen as straightforward alternatives to each other; instead, they may be combined in various ways and drawn on at different times. In this sense the strategies are better understood as representing the framework of different approaches that family members may use individually or collectively in coping with the diverse issues and contingencies they face.

As the name suggests, **open discussions** are the most explicit form of negotiation that Finch and Mason (1993) specify. These discussions involve family members coming together to consider a particular family issue openly, sometimes taking the form of a 'family conference' or else a series of linked discussions between different individuals. **Clear intentions** refers to processes where individuals themselves determine how they are going to act, but then convey this to other members of the network without much debate. Thus, an individual may decide they are (or are not) going to provide support for a relative, and act accordingly, without discussing this with any of the others involved. The final category, **non-decisions**, are – somewhat like clear intentions – implicit rather than explicit. However, a non-decision is distinctive in that decisions emerge without anyone apparently having formulated a clear intention or discussed it openly with others. Instead, the constellation of different people's circumstances and family 'biographies' are such that it becomes 'obvious' to all that a particular course of action is the one that will be followed (see Finch and Mason, 1993: chapter 3, for a full discussion of these different modes of negotiation).

While Finch and Mason's (1993) research is concerned principally with how decisions are reached over the appropriate provision of support and care for older parents who have become more infirm, the approach they take has far wider implications for understanding the nature of family relationships. In particular, their key argument that family relationships are constructed through interactive processes of negotiation and thus involve more than a simple following of culturally accepted rules has consequences for our understanding of a wide range of family behaviours. Their work emphasised the degree to which family members draw on their insider knowledge of each other's circumstances and biographies in determining what can reasonably be expected of one another in any given situation. By focusing on such issues as process, context, network, reputation and negotiation, Finch and Mason were at the forefront in emphasising agency in the construction of family relationships and in showing how important it is to see family interaction as emergent.

Family practices

These themes have a significant resonance with the approach developed by David Morgan (1996; 1999) in his discussion of family practices. Morgan uses the idea of family practices to portray the new realities of family experience. He seeks to emphasise that with the changes there have been in family living, thinking about 'the family' as a concrete entity or object is mistaken. To do so misrepresents the fluidity and flux of contemporary family experience, and furthermore misunderstands the forms of connection through which individuals are now tied to their families. What is required is a conception that is more open to the different levels of fluidity that operate within contemporary family forms. In a well-known passage, Morgan (1999: 16) writes: 'In this alternative approach, family [is] to be seen as less of a noun and more of an adjective or, possibly, a verb. "Family" represents a constructed quality of human interaction or an active process rather than a thing-like object of detached social investigation.'

Thus in introducing the concept of family practices, Morgan is concerned with furthering new understandings of family behaviour. Giving recognition to the increased fluidity of family life is one component of this, but there are other themes that Morgan also seeks to highlight through use of the term. As with Finch and Mason's (1993) work, acknowledging people's agency in constructing their family behaviour and relationships is particularly important. Rather than simply following established cultural principles or norms governing ways of doing and being family, Morgan sees individuals as active in creating their own modes of family living. In this, the idea of family practices communicates a strong sense of individuals collectively being active agents rather than passive recipients in the manufacture of their own family patterns. Like Beck's (1992: 129) notion of 'negotiated provisional family' to which Morgan (1999: 24) refers, the emphasis here is as much on participants' own desires and expectations as on external prescription.

While the notion of family practices recognises the freedoms that individuals have to create their own versions of family, it is equally successful in conveying the connection between such agency and aspects of structure. In other words, notwithstanding the variation there is in ways of doing family, conceptualising family interactions and relationships in terms of family practices recognises the significance of the everyday routines and agendas that characterise much family living. These 'regularities', as Morgan (1999: 17) terms them, covering the range of mundane activities from food consumption, household work schedules, leisure organisation and the like, are core to our understandings of 'family', yet shaped by the social and material realities with which we are confronted in our daily lives.

There are strong links between the idea of family practices and Nelson's (2006) work on single mothers 'doing family'. She too emphasises the degree of agency that people have in family matters, in her case with particular reference on ways of mothering. Importantly though, she also points out that mothering occurs within a network of relationships in which the others involved, especially the child's father and maternal grandmother, also have their own views about how mothering should be done. Moreover, like Morgan, Nelson highlights the fact that this interplay of agency occurs within cultural and material contexts that give shape and legitimacy to the different claims that are being made. Thus, in line with Finch and Mason's (1993) approach, the negotiations that arise around who has what authority to determine how children should be treated are informed by the material circumstances of the families (their housing standards, income level, occupational demands and so on) and by their cultural understandings of appropriate family and kinship responsibilities and behaviour. Agency is in play, but it is not a free-floating, disconnected agency.

As well as structure and agency, the concept of family practices also reflects the dialectic between stability and change inherent in contemporary family life. That is, while flux may be an increasingly common feature of family matters, family relationships are nonetheless routinely characterised by the continuity of established and taken-for-granted regularities (Charles et al, 2008). What happens today is generally similar to what happened yesterday or last week, and will be similar again tomorrow. At times, of course, family activities and relationships undergo radical disruption, through changing relational dynamics or under the pressure of specific external events. Yet such disruption is rare. At an everyday level, family living is marked more by continuity than by change, mainly because those involved are willing for it to be so. Their agency is not absent here, even if their choices are partially constrained by aspects of social and economic structure.

Rather, their agency is apparent in their continuing, if generally uncritical, adherence to the family practices they have established.

In drawing on the idea of family practices Morgan is clearly concerned with the routine activities that individuals and families are engaged in during the 'doing' of family matters – that is, matters that are pertinent to the realm of family. In the main this involves those activities that occur during family interactions and take place in the context of the home. However, it also includes other activities, such as the patterning of work and employment, which have an evident – and reciprocal – bearing on aspects of family living. In this regard, family practices are not somehow set apart from other spheres of activity or practice. Instead, what happens in families reflects the wider opportunities, choices and constraints that confront individuals as they make both their daily and more strategic decisions about the construction of their family lives.

Equally, as Morgan (1996) emphasises, the notion of family practices embraces more than just household practices. That is, while many aspects of family practices are rooted in the family as household, the term also incorporates the practices that tie the family as kinship together. This, of course, is particularly pertinent for this book. The relationships and connections that exist across generations, particularly between grandparents, parents and grandchildren, and how these develop over time and across different cohorts, are central issues for any analysis of people's family experiences. More than this, it is important to recognise that the family practices of later life incorporate the same properties as those that apply to the family practices of younger generations. Even if change in family life is less apparent than in earlier life phases when the formative transitions of childbirth, and partnership/household development and dissolution occur, fluidity and flux still mark older people's family experiences.

Family practices are inevitably shaped by core family events such as children leaving home, grandchildren being born, retirement from employment, episodes of illness and infirmity and, ultimately, widow(er)hood, even if the timing of these has altered over time. Moreover the flux that there is in the family arrangements and relationships of younger – and, for that matter, surviving older – generations also has an impact on the family experiences of people in later life. As an obvious example, given the commitment and solidarity typically evident across generations, a child's separation and divorce, especially if there are grandchildren involved, is liable to have direct consequences for a parent's family practices. Other less extreme changes in adult children's lives, such as geographical mobility, changing patterns of work and employment, and indeed the very process of ageing, will also influence the family practices of the older generation (see for example Chapters Seven and Eight).

Important here is that the ways that people in later life respond to the mundane and more exceptional flux of family life are no more determined than they are for younger cohorts. The older people too have agency; they too will make decisions about how they want to react to different family contingencies. Like younger cohorts, they are also active in constructing and reconstructing the ways that they do their family relationships, both within the home and outside it. This is often downplayed in popular understandings of older people's family lives, and sometimes in academic analyses too. Rather, older people are portrayed as exercising little choice and having little control, merely reacting in more or less set ways to whatever issues they happen to be facing. Of course some older people do have little choice or control over their lives, in particular when their levels of disability and dependency are high. However, the great majority of people in later life are no more dependent socially or economically than are younger cohorts. Like the latter, they are likely to be involved in a range of interdependencies with others, including family members inside and outside their households. But, within the constraints of their material circumstances, they still have just as much agency over their lifestyle choices as do younger cohorts.

Multigenerational bonds in a changing family context

The greater fluidity and diversity that has been a feature of family relationships over the last 30 years or so has had a direct effect on many older people. They too may have experienced separation and divorce, created partnerships outside marriage and formed stepfamilies, as well as living through their children's, and in some cases, their grandchildren's, changing family circumstances. The multigenerational consequences of these changes are not always given the same recognition as the impact these changes have on the patterning of households. Partnership creation and dissolution clearly do have profound consequences for what, as above, we can term the organisation of family as household relationships, as well as on the patterning of individual lifecourses. However, collectively they can also have a significant effect on family as kinship ties, resulting in constellations of kinship solidarities that take a quite different form to those regarded as standard during much of the mid–20th century.

This is a theme developed by Vern Bengtson (2001) in his argument that multigenerational family bonds are becoming increasingly significant in family life, given the types of change that are occurring in partnership patterns with late modernity. But Bengtson relates this to two further demographic features of contemporary life – the increase in life expectancy over the past 100 years and decreasing levels of fertility. As a result, Bengtson (2001: 5) argues, not only has a 'beanpole' family structure emerged, 'representing more family generations alive but with fewer members in each generation', but, more significantly, people are now experiencing 'cosurvivorship between generations' (2001: 6) for longer periods. In particular, many more people than in previous eras are now involved in prolonged grandparental relationships, both as grandchildren and as grandparents, with many also experiencing some period of great-grandparenthood. While this may be modified slightly by the cumulative effect of increases in age of first childbearing occurring since the late 1970s, it represents a significant development in terms of family and lifecourse phases. Moreover, as Bengtson points out, in the context of changing patterns of partnership commitment, it also has implications for the understandings that social researchers develop of family organisation.

On the basis of these considerations, Bengtson (2001: 5) argues that 'Relations across more than two generations are becoming increasingly important to individuals and families in American society.' While he is explicitly referring to the US here, the issues he raises apply more generally across western societies. More contentiously, he further suggests that for many people multigenerational bonds may be becoming 'more important than nuclear family ties for well-being and support over the course of their lives' (Bengtson, 2001: 5). While we will not be concerned in this book with whether a family form typified by strong multigenerational solidarities is now of greater consequence in people's lives than more narrowly defined nuclear family solidarities, we fully agree with Bengtson that adequate understandings of contemporary family life do require a focus that embraces a generational – and consequently a lifecourse – perspective.

A generational and lifecourse perspective entails a fuller recognition than is sometimes apparent in other family frameworks of the ways in which each individual's life trajectory is inevitably bound up with the circumstances of others in their families. That is, it sees family life as being made up of a network of relationships, developing over time and generally across households, which pattern in a variety of ways the experiences of the different individuals involved. In Crosnoe and Elder's (2002: 1089) terms, lifecourse theory draws attention to 'the importance of family members' linked lives'. Thus it serves to emphasise the dynamic character of family relationships, as well as the changing socio-historic and socio-economic contexts in which these 'linked lives' are constructed. In these regards, the premises informing lifecourse theory are clearly compatible with the ideas of negotiation and family practices introduced earlier in this chapter.

It can of course be argued that in Britain the importance of generational ties in family and kinship behaviour has long been recognised. The classic family studies of the mid-20th century were at pains to point this out (eg Young and Willmott, 1957; Rosser and Harris, 1965; Bell, 1968; see also Phillipson et al, 2001; Charles et al, 2008). What is new now, though – in line with the arguments made throughout this chapter – is the greater diversity currently found in the organisation of generational relationships, both across the population and individually over the lifecourse. In other words, while many of the debates around family issues, both within sociology and more generally, have concerned partnerships and the parenting of young children, the increasing fluidity of family networks and family practices has also framed people's experiences of generational relationships.

The diversity that exists in generational relationships is evident in research on grandparenting. As these studies show, there are many different patterns of grandparent–grandchild involvement, some linked to factors such as gender and ethnicity, others more to do with personality and agency. Some grandparents are highly active in their grandchildren's lives, others are seen only intermittently (Crosnoe and Elder, 2002; Dench and Ogg, 2002). Some are willing to provide significant levels of support, while others prioritise generational independence more (Mason et al, 2007). Moreover, the patterns of commitment and solidarity change over time as the circumstances of the generations, including the age of the grandchildren, alter. At certain points in the lifecourse, for example when the grandchildren are young or when a parental partnership ends, grandparents are likely to provide higher levels of material and emotional support. At other times there will be less need for explicit support, with generational solidarity being expressed through the mundane routines established over time for sustaining involvement in each other's lives (see Chapter Six).

In line with the issues discussed earlier in this chapter, generational relationships involve agency and negotiation as well as normative constraint and structure. People exercise elements of choice over these relationships, as they do over partnerships and other family ties. As above, some people desire more intergenerational family involvement than others, and desire more at different times. Some ties have higher levels of exchange and reciprocity than others. Equally, as Connidis and McMullin (2002) and Bengtson et al (2002) have more recently debated, the character of solidarity between the generations is not necessarily consistently positive, even in ties where all parties would agree that the relationships are close. Close ties frequently – indeed inevitably – contain their own ambiguities, at times involving ambivalent, if not contradictory, feelings and behaviour. At different times, conflict can emerge, more readily in some relationships than in others. Bengtson's (2001:8) own model of solidarity in intergenerational relationships highlights the different dimensions there are to such solidarity and recognises that each dimension has positive and negative poles. Furthermore, the different individuals involved in the relationship (directly and indirectly) can be seen to have their own distinct locations on these dimensions.

Thus the patterning of these relationships is obviously not just a matter of individual choice. The organisation of these relationships is a mutual, interactive accomplishment. In Finch and Mason's (1993) terms, these relationships result from the generally implicit negotiations that occur between all those involved about how they want their relationships to be patterned, with the histories of the different relationships clearly providing a background that influences current negotiations. And in Morgan's (1996) sense, the family practices that develop around these relationships emerge over time as a consequence of the understandings that the different actors reach about the structuring of their relationships. But as Morgan emphasises, these emergent understandings are also patterned by the (often different) normative beliefs and material circumstances of those involved.

Despite this emphasis on choice, it is worth recognising that most generational family relationships do involve a continuing commitment and solidarity, even though this is expressed in diverse ways. In other words, there tends to be a cultural assumption that parent–child relationships, and in turn grandparent–grandchild ties, should be sustained throughout the lifecourse. The relationships may not always be harmonious, sometimes there may be rifts; nonetheless they are understood as rightly entailing a lifelong involvement. In this, they encapsulate the 'diffuse, enduring solidarity' that David Schneider (1968) saw as central to

American kinship some 40 years ago. There is acknowledged variation in their practice, but over the lifecourse, relationships between parents and children – and in turn between grandparents and grandchildren – typically demonstrate a strong and continuing concern for each other's welfare. In an era characterised by increased partnership fluidity, it is this that Bengtson (2001) is reflecting when he argues that multigenerational bonds are of increasing significance in contemporary family structures.

Family practices in later life

The family experiences of older people are frequently analysed in terms of social problems and personal dependency. The framework used is often one in which older people's increasing infirmity and a heightened reliance on others tends to dominate. Our approach in this book is somewhat different. We want to examine the family relations of older people in the round. We want to recognise that older people's family relations are not dominated by a 'care' or 'dependency' perspective. Of course, the need for support can become a key issue for some older people for some (usually short) period of their lives. For most older people most of the time, however, this does not provide the touchstone of their family lives.

Instead, as is true across the lifecourse, most older people are involved in a wide range of family practices involving different exchanges and different interdependencies. These necessarily shift and change with time, as different people within the family network move into different positions in the family and acquire different responsibilities. As we have emphasised in this chapter, the greater flux evident in contemporary family relationships has an effect on the family experiences of older and younger people. To examine these shifts and to understand the range of family exchanges in which older people are routinely involved, it is necessary to focus on the types of process that are encapsulated in the perspectives discussed in this chapter. In particular, older people need to be seen as active in the construction of their family lives rather than passive. Understanding the character of the family relationships in which they are involved requires a focus on agency as well as on normative assumption and structural location. As concepts such as 'negotiation', 'family practices' and 'doing family' illustrate, family relationships do not just happen in later life. They are actively constructed by those involved, through their interaction over time.

At the same time, family practices are produced within the social and economic contexts that pattern people's experiences. The material circumstances of people's lives are key elements within this, not least in later life when pension deficiencies may be particularly constraining. But as emphasised above, it is also important to consider broader family circumstances, with both lifecourse and family network characteristics being of consequence. Thus, if we are to understand older people's family relationships, it is important to locate them within a developmental framework. The nature of their family practices in earlier periods of their lives – with their spouses, with their children, with their siblings – influences the character of these relationships in later life. Of course, these relationships change over time, but always within the context of what went before. Similarly as we have also stressed above, the family relationships that people sustain in different life phases, including older age, are not solely dyadic. Families comprise networks of relationships that are mutually influencing, as the work of the authors discussed above attests.

In the chapters that follow we will explore more precisely how the themes discussed in this chapter shape older people's different family experiences.

TWO

Families in later life

Introduction

Understanding family practices in later life raises a number of difficulties for research and the development of social policy. Three main problems can be identified from a survey of the literature provided by historians, sociologists and those working in the field of social policy. First, generalisations are often made about 'the family' in previous centuries or in 'modern times'. These often ignore substantial class, gender and ethnic differences – strikingly apparent in the 21st century but no less real at earlier periods of historical time (Pelling and Smith, 1991; Haber and Gratton, 1994). Second, certain types of data are problematic if we want to draw well-founded assessments of attitudes and practices towards older people within the family. Census material may be admirable for some purposes (for determining the structure of households, to take one illustration) but less adequate for others (for assessing motives behind support for older kin, for example). Diaries, narrative interviews, archival records and policy documents also have merits and limitations for understanding the family as a 'set of practices' as opposed to a 'rule-bound' social institution (see Chapter One). Third, and probably most importantly, as an area of study, research on the family has been particularly affected by value positions about the nature of social change and its impact on family life and family practices.

Perspectives on the family and older people tend, as Kertzer (1995) has observed, to swing between two extremes: the 'romantic view' of the past, which views older people as firmly in control of their lives, treated with respect by all around them, and the 'revisionist view', which sees older people shunted into workhouses, ejected by their families at the first sign of frailty and dependency. In social theory, the former approach was illustrated by modernisation theory as developed by Cowgill and Holmes (1972), which associated technological and industrial development with a lowering of the status of older people. In the case of the latter, historians such as Lawrence Stone (1977) viewed the rise of poor relief as a sign of the family transferring responsibility to the community. Referring to the later 18th century he suggested that: 'The fate of King Lear at the hands of his daughter foreshadowed a century of change and uncertainty in family and societal attitudes to older people' (Stone, 1977: 403–4).

As might be surmised from the above, studies about the role of family relationships in later life have attracted a rich literature, from a variety of disciplinary perspectives. Sociological interest – notably in the US – has always been strong, reflected in debates in the 1950s and 1960s about the emergence of the 'modified extended family' (Litwak, 1960), and its role in exchanging support between nuclear families. In the British context, Townsend (1957) confirmed the central place of older people in the family, a finding subsequently reinforced in research comparing Denmark, Britain and the US (Shanas et al, 1968). Historians took slightly longer to discover old age as a topic (Stearns, 1977), but with the influence of Laslett (1977; 1984) in particular a rapid growth of interest came in the 1980s, with the historical demography of old age a notable area of investigation (Wall, 1984). Social theory applied to the family in old age has also been a significant subject for discussion, led in the US by Bengtson (2001) with his work on 'multigenerational families' (see further below and Chapter One). Demographers have also made significant advances in furthering understanding about family life, especially in areas such as changes in household structure, the impact of internal migration and changes in kinship behaviour (Grundy, 1999; Murphy, 2004).

The purpose of this chapter is to review the development of research on the family in later life, tracing continuities as well as discontinuities, taking a range of different types of studies. To consider these issues the chapter is divided into four major sections: first, relevant historical findings relating to family relationships in later life are reviewed; second, key findings from the sociological literature are assessed; third, areas of change in family and personal relationships are summarised; fourth, the impact of social exclusion on relationships in old age is examined.

Older people in history

Family life was certainly a major part of growing old in previous centuries – that much at least can be stated from numerous studies of pre-industrial and early modern Europe and America. Peter Laslett (1977), writing about the 17th century, highlighted the importance of factors such as delayed marriage and women giving birth in their 30s and 40s, resulting in the likelihood of a child still being at home when a parent entered old age. Research by Fischer (1977), covering 17th- and 18th-century America, also noted the consequences of high fertility, with the youngest child often not marrying until parents were into their 60s. The role of unmarried children in providing care is an important theme in historical research (Ottaway, 2004). Robin's (1984) study of a 19th-century Devon parish found more than one-third of people aged 70–79 still had an unmarried child at home, these children performing a significant role in the care of their parents.

The residential experience of older people illustrates a variety of trends. Research in the British context demonstrates a decline over the last four centuries in the frequency with which married and non-married older people live with their children. Continuities in residential behaviour should, though, be noted. The proportion of older people living in institutions has been surprisingly constant (at between 3% and 6%) over the past four hundred years. A substantial number of older people (women especially) have always lived alone: studies of English communities in the period 1684–1796 show around 15% of women aged 65 and over doing so. Richard Wall (1998) stresses continuities in the household structures of older people over several centuries, but with the transformation towards independent households gathering pace from the early 1960s onwards, with an increase in those living alone, and a corresponding decline in those living with people other than their spouse. By the 1990s, 5% of older people in Britain lived with a child, in comparison with 40% at the start of the 1950s.

Similar trends can be illustrated from the example of the US. In 1900, more than 60% of all of those aged 65 and over resided with one or more of their (usually unmarried) children. Haber and Gratton (1994: 44) observe: 'Whether as a household head or as a dependent of their offspring, the elderly shared residences with the young, uniting their assets and abilities as well as their conflicts.' As in the case of Britain, improved personal resources, as well as greater options in respect of housing, facilitated the development of separate residences. Haber and Gratton (1994) note that the provision of Social Security brought two important trends: steep declines in complex living arrangements, and corresponding increases in independent, autonomous households. By 1962, the proportion of older Americans who lived with their children had dropped to 25% and by 1975 to 14%.

More generally, the evidence suggests – for the past and present – a desire among older people to maintain their own household for as long as possible (Thane, 2000). Even with the death of a partner, the evidence suggests that widows or (more rarely) widowers tried to maintain their own household for as long as possible – 'intimacy at a distance', to use the revealing phrase of Rosenmayr and Kockeis (1963). Laslett (1977: 213) supports this in the pre-industrial context as follows: 'The conclusion might be that then, as now, a place of your own, with help in the house, with access to your children, within reach of support might have been what the elderly and aged most wanted for themselves.'

The likelihood of older people moving into the homes of married children was, however, limited for reasons other than custom or sentiment. At least one in three of those entering old age would have no surviving children with whom they might have lived (Thomson, 1986). For those with children still alive, the migration of the children (especially from rural into expanding industrial areas) would further reduce opportunities for co-residence. As for care provided by family members, it must also be acknowledged that there is no clear evidence for a 'binding cultural norm' (Hanawalt, 1986) that care would be received. Thane (see, further, Ottaway, 2004) elaborates on this:

> [T]here was a strong obligation on individuals to give what material and emotional support they could to elderly relatives, even if they did not live in the same household; but only within reason, and not if by doing so they would impoverish themselves or their families. The obligations of married sons and daughters were first to their spouses and their children and only secondarily, if they had resources to spare, for their parents. (Thane, 2000: 145)

The limits to familial obligations were reflected in the English Poor Law, with children alone having a legal duty to offer assistance to impoverished parents. Even here prosecutions for failing to provide help were rare and, according to Thomson,

> pressed with the greatest reluctance; were seldom successful ... were not often complied with by the few sons who did have an order made against them ... Single daughters do not appear to have been considered as bearing a responsibility, at least before the 1870s; maintenance orders were almost invariably for tiny, token amounts ordered as a matter of principle rather than as a real reimbursement of the community's expenses. (Thomson, 1991: 199)

Thomson (1991: 199) concludes from this that: 'The whole leaves the overwhelming impression that everyone involved – magistrates, poor law officers, the families of the poor, the elderly themselves – found this a distressing and offensive business. Quite simply, it was "unenglish" behaviour to expect children to support parents.'

None of this should detract from the evidence of substantial support being provided by children to older parents. Ottaway (2004: 155) stresses from her review of family life in 18th-century England that: 'Children were, indeed, of vital importance to the well-being of their aged mothers and fathers.' Moreover, the support of unmarried children was probably crucial for many older people in helping them maintain 'independent' households. However, it is equally important to emphasise support that flowed down as well as up the generational chain (see below). The context in which help was provided is also important in understanding the limitations placed upon support within the family. Ottaway provides helpful background here:

> The family history of old people reveals the reciprocity of family relationships and the contributions of the elderly to their children. Moreover, it seems clear that those old men and women who were most in need of assistance (the aged poor) had children who were unlikely to have the wherewithal to offer them support. Within this context it seems unhelpful that so much attention within the historiography as well as within popular culture has focused on the question 'Did children in the past care for their elderly parents'. (Ottaway, 2004: 155)

Families in later life: sources of continuity

If the question of whether children cared for older people in the past has been of considerable interest to historians, the issue of whether they care in the present has preoccupied those concerned with sociology, social policy and related disciplines.

But the context that informs the work of social scientists as opposed to historians is rather different. This was sketched in the previous chapter in terms of the fluidity and diversity that now characterise family relationships, linked to the growth of multigenerational ties and support from individuals not formerly defined as kin. As the previous section highlighted, much has changed, especially over the past 50 years, in respect of co-residence and living arrangements experienced by older people. But how much has this also transformed attitudes and behaviour towards the care of older people?

One approach to answering this question is to compare findings from research on the family carried out in the period following the Second World War with studies from the late 20th and early 21st centuries. Research in the late 1940s and 1950s provided important insights into the lives of older people.[1] This research, much of it linked to the Institute for Community Studies led by Michael Young, examined how far family ties were being replaced by the various services associated with the new welfare state. Most of the studies in fact demonstrated the continuing importance of kinship and family life in post-war Britain. Sheldon (1948), for example, in his survey of Wolverhampton, found older people to be an essential part of family life. He questioned whether the phrase 'living alone' had any real meaning, given the high degree of residential proximity of kin to older people. Townsend (1957), in his influential study of family life in the London Borough of Bethnal Green (now part of Tower Hamlets), found a community in which older people were heavily engaged in various supportive roles within the family (see also Young and Willmott, 1957). In the largely middle-class suburb of Woodford and Wanstead (in Essex), Willmott and Young (1960: 38) reached the conclusion that: 'The old people of the suburb are plainly as much in touch with children ... as those in the East End.' The family, then, appeared to have retained its significance for older people. Townsend (1957: 210) expressed this: 'To the old person as much as the young it [the family] seems to be the supreme comfort and support. Its central purpose is as strong as ever.'

How many of the conclusions from research in the 1940s and 1950s are still relevant in the vastly different context of the 21st century? Major changes have of course taken place – not least in terms of the living arrangements of older people. The change here has been from households often with two or more generations (typically older people sharing with one of their children or children-in-law) to predominantly single-generation households. Older people living in households with two or more generations were relatively common in the early post-war era: 51% of older people lived in this way in Wolverhampton in 1945; 41% in Bethnal Green in 1954/5. In contrast, the norm today is for older people to live either with a spouse or on their own – as a single-generation household. The 2001 Census showed that of older people living in the community, 92% lived in single-generation households, either living alone or with one or more other older person, usually his/her spouse or more rarely a sibling.

There are, however, important ethnic differences in respect of household living arrangements. Soule et al (2005) summarise variations in those living in complex households (that is, arrangements that are not independent living or as a couple only). The 2001 Census showed 12% of White men aged 85 and over lived in a complex household, compared with 42% of Asians and 29% of Chinese or other ethnic groups. Among women, the equivalent figures were: 19%, 68% and 47%.

Living alone in old age was certainly much less common 50 years ago: just 10% of older people lived this way in Wolverhampton in 1945; and 25% in Bethnal Green in 1954/5. By the mid-1990s, both areas had seen an increase to around one in three older people. Nationally, the 2001 Census found 37% of older people living alone. Gender and age variations are important here, however, with 60% of women aged 75 and over now living alone, compared with 29% of men of the same age.

Research 50 years ago also emphasised the extent of geographical closeness between older people and their kin. In Wolverhampton in the late 1940s, one-third of older people had relatives living within a mile, with 4% having a child living next door. In Bethnal Green in the early 1950s, the average older person had 13 relatives living within a mile; 53% of older people had a married child living either in the same dwelling or within five minutes' walk.

In comparison with 50 years ago, multigenerational households are now rare (except for within some ethnic minority groups), and the typical experience in old age is to live alone or with just one other person. But to what extent has this changed the family life of older people? In some respects, the evidence from numerous studies would suggest a considerable degree of continuity in the ties maintained between generations. Research suggests that the majority of older people remain part of a substantial kin network comprising spouses/partners, children, grandchildren and siblings (Phillipson et al, 2001). Close relationships are now more geographically dispersed than the examples given above, although a survey conducted in Britain in 1999 found around half those aged over 50 had non-resident children living within 30 minutes' travel time (Grundy et al, 1999). Levels of interaction between older people and their children and other relatives remain extensive. A survey published in 2004 reported that three-quarters of older people (77%) saw relatives at least weekly, with just around one in ten seeing relatives less than once a year (Victor et al, 2004). The family remains a crucial source of support to older people when there are particular needs in respect of household tasks, help when ill, and talking over emotional problems. The following three quotes from people talking about the support provided by their family illustrate the above themes (Phillipson et al, 2001: 64, 71, 73):

> Oh I think that family life is 100% important ... in every way ... because I mean for myself now this ... I have only got one son right, there is peace of mind. I was under the weather, the wife had a very bad spell and so family then was ... It showed family life, everybody was prepared to ... I mean at the drop of a hat they would be there ... anything on the phone. I mean my son has got a car and we have got their phone numbers, posted up down there and that to us is ...

It doesn't matter what time of the day or night, if there is a problem, pick the phone up ... so you know family life is very, very important. (Mr Green, aged 75, living with his wife)

I thought I wasn't quite ready to look for a retirement home, depending on how my cancer was going to progress. So it was decided that I come here to my daughter's. Well my other daughter lives very near as well so I mean she will take me to the shops sometimes, she will take me to the Post Office to collect my pension and I will go and spend a day with her now and again. (Mrs Harris, aged 81, widow)

Ken, the elder one ... he lives [about seven miles away] ... Jill has recently moved and she is about four miles away. So ... she always comes as she has done for ages to take me up to the Post Office on pension day and do what shopping I need while she is here you see. (Mr Ellis, aged 91, widower)

The above quotations focus upon assistance provided *for* older people. In contrast, research by Ottaway (2004: 155) on the English family in the 18th century highlighted the degree to which support provided by parents *to* their children 'utterly dwarf[ed] the assistance that flowed up from the younger generation'. This finding is replicated in contemporary research on intergenerational ties, for example in that reported by Arber and Attias-Donfut (2000), Bonvalet and Ogg (2007) and Hoff and Tesch-Römer (2007). Hoff and Tesch-Römer (2007: 73) suggest that 'The reliability of intergenerational relations has proved to be highly dependable and stable in the last decades. Parent/child relations are characterized by a high degree of mutual exchange, including financial, instrumental and social support.'

Contrary to predictions of conflict between 'welfare generations'– a consistent theme in neoliberal thought in the 1980s and 1990s – generations appeared to be maintaining their commitment to each other, through what Kohli and his co-researchers (2000) referred to as multidimensional forms of exchange. In France, Attias-Donfut and Wolff (2000) demonstrated the role of the 'pivot' (middle-aged) generation in providing economic support to young people on the threshold to adulthood. Importantly, these researchers demonstrated the ways in which public transfers reinforced rather than weakened family solidarity. This interweaving of the public and private is presented as follows:

Within the life course, individuals begin by receiving support from their mid-life parents which they in turn indirectly repay in their economically active years through their provision of pensions. During this period they also provide to their adult children and receive private transfers from their elderly parents who in turn benefit from care as they enter later life. (Attias-Donfut and Wolff, 2000: 65)

Cross-national variations in family relationships require further investigation although the OASIS research in five European countries has provided a wealth of information (Lowenstein and Daatland, 2006; see also Fokkema et al, 2008).[2] This research explored attitudes to care for older people among a sample of adults aged 25–74 and 75 and over. Support for filial norms broadly followed a north–south gradient, being highest in Spain and Israel; somewhat lower in Norway, England and Germany. The residential proximity of adult children and their parents showed a similar north–south variation, greatest in Spain and Israel and least in Norway. While the majority in Spain and Israel agreed that adult children ought to live near their parents, the English and more particularly the Norwegians put greater emphasis on 'independent living' (Daatland and Herlofson, 2003). More generally, the research confirmed that the existence of a welfare state was entirely compatible with family support for older people:

> Filial solidarity is not incompatible with generous welfare state arrangements, nor do filial obligations imply that relatives are seen as 'natural' care providers. Welfare state expansion has not eroded filial obligations, and indeed many of those who strongly advocate filial responsibility also believe that it is formal services that should be primarily responsible for care provision. (Daatland and Herlofson, 2003: 556)

Families in later life: sources of change

As well as identifying continuities over time, changes in the structure of family relations in old age must also be emphasised. Of particular importance here, as highlighted in Chapter One, is the multigenerational family and its influence on roles and activities in later life. The increased prevalence of families with three, four and even five living generations represents a substantial change in family life, the emergence of the grandparenting role (see Chapter Six) being one illustration of this. A British survey conducted in 1999 found that most adults were members of a family with three living generations (Grundy et al, 1999). Leach et al (2008) in their study of the first 'baby boom' generation (those born 1945–54) found 43% of those aged 50–57 had a mother alive (average age 79.8 years)and 20% had a father alive (average age 80.7). Setting this besides lower rates of childlessness for this cohort, the authors highlight the possibility of a 'sandwiched generation' of boomers caring for grandchildren on the one side and older parents on the other.

Grundy and Henretta (2006: 709) make the point that resolving conflicting expectations from ascending and descending generations is a key issue for the three-generation family. We know relatively little about how competing demands from children (who may still be partly dependent on parents entering late middle age) and older parents are managed. Grundy and Henretta (2006) examined two important questions relating to this issue: How do mid-life adults divide their efforts between helping older parents and adult children? Does the provision of help to parents reduce the likelihood of helping children (and vice versa)? In fact, the evidence, drawing upon data sets from the UK and US, suggested that, independent of demographic, health or other characteristics, those who help the ascendent generation will also help the descendent generation and vice versa. In other words, there is a form of 'family solidarity' at work whereby 'those with the strongest solidarity tend to assist both generations ... while those with low solidarity are least likely to help multiple generations' (Grundy and Henretta, 2006: 710). However, there is limited understanding of the social characteristics associated with each and the factors strengthening or weakening supportive ties.

Another source of change concerns the type of relationships maintained in old age. Older people as part of a couple with a relationship of 40 or more years is now a commonplace experience. In addition, older people (men especially) see their partner both as a confidant and a source of support in times of crisis. This is almost certainly not a new development, but one that stands out more prominently in the lives of people studied in the late 20th and early 21st centuries (see Chapter Four).

Another important change is the significant role played by friends in the lives of older people. Family and kinship ties remain important but they are not the only relationships maintained. Friendships – especially those sustained for a substantial period of the lifecourse – may provide emotional support and even practical forms of assistance (Adams and Blieszner, 1989; Phillipson et al, 2001). They may be especially prominent in the networks of those widowed, childless or single, and among those drawn from middle class and professional groups. This appears to be the case with the current cohort of older people and may be even more characteristic of future cohorts. While some older people remain attached to what in the 1960s Frankenburg (1966: 93) defined as an 'environment of kinship', many are also connected to networks of 'choice' consisting of ties to friends, leisure associates and neighbours, as well as family relationships (see Spencer and Pahl, 2006).

At the same time, a minority of older people experience a degree of alienation from family and community ties. Of particular relevance is that some older men who divorced when their children were young became estranged from these now adult children as a result of the 'clean break' nature of many divorces until quite late in the mid-20th century (Burgoyne and Clark, 1984). Some remarried and had second families, but others did not. Increasing levels of divorce may continue to produce long-term tensions across the generations, though with contemporary marital separation and divorce there is increasing emphasis on the importance of maintaining the parental relationship rather than adopting a 'clean break' strategy. Nonetheless, as discussed elsewhere in this book, the diversity of current marriage and partnership behaviour is likely to be reflected in more diverse personal networks in later life. Indeed it is likely that non-kin ties will generally play a more prominent role in later life in the future.

Patterns of exclusion in later life

Despite the supportive ties experienced by a majority of older people, substantial groups also experience problems of loneliness and social exclusion, reflecting vulnerabilities of class, gender and ethnicity as experienced through the lifecourse. Family life continues to be important to the majority of older people, but it may also be influenced by pressures associated with poverty and various forms of social exclusion – these have a marked effect on the quality of relationships experienced in old age.

A range of studies from the 1940s up until the present time have identified that between 5% and 10% of older people perceive themselves as lonely all, or most of the time (Victor et al, 2002). Research in this area suggests an increase over time in the proportion of older people reporting to be 'sometimes lonely'. Work carried out in 2001 (Victor et al, 2002) found that nearly one in three (32%) of older people fell into this category, a much higher figure than that reported in previous surveys. High rates of loneliness have also been reported in a study of older people living in areas of severe deprivation (mostly inner-city wards) in England. This study reported 44% of older people to be 'moderately lonely' and no less than 16% to be experiencing 'severe' or 'very severe' loneliness (Scharf et al, 2002).

Older people may experience more general problems of exclusion arising from poverty, pressures arising from social change and difficulties with managing chronic ill-health (Office of the Deputy Prime Minister, 2006). Research in areas characterised by severe deprivation (as measured by relevant government indicators) in Liverpool, Manchester and the London Borough of Newham found that older people were at least twice as likely to experience poverty as those in Britain as a whole – 45% were in poverty, compared with 21% in a national study using similar measures (Scharf et al, 2002).

Although the majority of older people in these inner-city communities had access to basics such as two meals a day and were part of an active network of family and friends, relatively high proportions struggled to afford what most would regard as necessities of life. For example, around one in three of those interviewed in each area were unable to make regular savings, to replace worn-out furniture, to replace or repair broken electrical goods or to take a holiday away from home for one week a year. The following quotations illustrate the daily lives of three respondents managing daily life on a low income (Scharf et al, 2005: 17).

> It [the state pension] doesn't give the opportunity of buying luxuries if you know what I mean. I mean I couldn't go out and afford a lump of steak or the meat. You just buy things within reason, like sausages, the cheaper brand of stuff. (Mrs Richards, aged 85, widow living alone)

> Well I know what I want and it's all within reason. But the £30
> I've got left from the state pension doesn't keep me in shopping ... I
> can't afford luxuries really. I mean like getting a bottle of whiskey or
> something like that ... I couldn't do that. (Mr Lee, aged 85, widower
> living alone)

> I got to buy the things I can afford ... Things are so dear in the shop
> and sometimes I have to leave some things, buy smaller one, you know
> just buy what you can afford ... say you want sugar, they have 3 or 4
> different kinds of sugar and you have to take the cheaper one because
> they [are] dear, they have cheap things and dear things. Well the thing
> I hate to have is cheap things. I don't like anything cheap to eat. I'll
> wear [i.e. cheap clothes] but I couldn't eat it. So I just buy a small
> amount. (Mrs Walker, aged 74, widow living with son)

Certain groups may be especially vulnerable to poverty and other types of
exclusion in old age. The young adults who migrated to Britain in the 1950s
from the Caribbean and Indian subcontinent are now reaching old age, but
often in difficult financial and personal circumstances. On the one side, some
research suggests that older people from ethnic minorities do relatively well in
terms of family and social networks, reflecting the investment by this generation
in building a neighbourhood-based ethnic community (Nazroo et al, 2004). On
the other hand, groups such as Pakistanis and Bangladeshis are much more likely
to have experienced being unemployed in the period leading up to retirement,
to have chronic ill-health, and to live in poverty in old age. More than 90% of
Bangladeshi and 75% of Pakistani households with one or more members aged
50 or more are in the bottom income quintile, compared with just over a third
of equivalent English households.

A study of older people living in inner-city communities recorded very high
levels of poverty among certain minority ethnic groups, notably Somalis (77%
in poverty) and Pakistanis (67%) (Scharf et al, 2002). The case of Saeed Raza and
his wife is typical of the pressures arising from limited financial resources. The
couple have lived in Manchester for over 30 years since moving from Pakistan. In
retirement Mr Raza finds the task of making ends meet particularly stressful: 'I find
it really hard. Sometimes I stay awake at night thinking about how we will pay
these bills and manage with what we are on. I feel so helpless.' When asked if he
goes without necessities, Mr Raza replied: 'All the time! Do you know, I haven't
bought any new clothes for myself for the last year. My shoes are wearing down,
my clothes are thinning and don't keep out the cold as much. But we need the
money to buy food and pay our bills' (Scharf et al, 2004: 42-3).

Experiences such as the above are likely to become more common, given
pressures associated with higher levels of unemployment and the low level of
income from supplementary pensions (Phillipson, 2009). Older people – notably
women and those from particular ethnic minority groups – are likely to face

new vulnerabilities associated with poverty and poor housing. Understanding the effect of these on family relationships in old age will become a crucial issue for researchers to address.

Conclusion

One broad conclusion to the state of family relations has been offered by Hoff and Tesch-Römer (2007: 77): 'The relative importance of family relations and family support in contemporary Western societies may have diminished, but as empirical findings of many studies into the [subject] have shown, family relations have remained a reliable and stable source of support, despite publicly provided support alternatives.' Moreover, they go on to make the point that, notwithstanding comprehensive welfare systems, older generations have maintained their role in distributing resources down through the generational chain – to their own children as well as to grandchildren.

Such a finding confirms the historical evidence cited earlier and indicates significant continuities in the provision of family support. But the changes are also important to note and will be highlighted at different points in this book. Thus, as is argued in Chapter Eight, families increasingly need to be understood in a transnational context; in many instances this places major constraints on the provision of care by close family members. And to reiterate the point emphasised in Chapter One, 'the family' is an increasingly diverse and fluid institution, reflecting a greater range of family practices and behaviours than may historically have been the case. In part, of course, that is because older people are themselves a much more varied group – whether defined in terms of different birth cohorts, the expectations of different social classes, or the attitudes of particular minority ethnic groups. These, and other social characteristics, play a major role in determining the quality of life of older people and the nature of the support that they give and receive. The remaining chapters of this book will explore further the differences as well as similarities in the family life of older people.

Notes
[1] Some of the key studies in this tradition include Sheldon (1948), Townsend (1957) and Young and Willmott (1957).

[2] Old Age and Autonomy: The Role of Service Systems and Inter-generational Family Solidarity (OASIS) Research Project was funded by the European Commission 5th Framework Research and Development Programme 'Quality of Life'.

THREE

Older parents and their adult children

Introduction

There has been a tendency in the UK, North America and indeed Western Europe for politicians, policy makers, researchers and, equally important, the public to view the relationship between ageing parents and their adult children[1] in a very narrow way as one that is dominated by care-giving and/or care receiving. Whilst recognising the vital importance of the welfare role undertaken within families, Matthews (2002: 211) warns that one consequence of the '… myopia of focusing entirely on family caregivers' has been to produce a gloomy picture of older families. More recently in the UK, a popular Saturday newspaper published a two-page feature (Hilpern, 2008), 'Who's going to take care of Mum?', that explored the 'plight' of older adults who were left to care for their ageing parents. Furthermore, the theorising of intergenerational relationships discussed in Chapter One, specifically those perspectives that relate to relationships between adult child and older parent such as solidarity, reciprocity, conflict and ambivalence, have been so extensively employed within studies on relationships of welfare (see for example, the cross-national OASIS study) that it would be all too easy to forget their relevance and usefulness for all aspects of intergenerational family life.

Indeed, as Connidis (2001: 158) reminds us, most older people maintain relatively independent lifestyles for most, if not all, of their lives, and most of those older people are enmeshed in a diversity of family relationships not just those relating to 'welfare'. Although a minority of older people are 'childless', that is either have never had children or have experienced the death of a child during their lifecourse, most older people in the UK are parents and many of them have adult children who themselves are approaching what might be termed pensionable age (ONS, 2001). Changes in demographic trends over the last 50 years, brought about by improvement in and access to public health measures, decreased mortality and fertility (Phillipson, 1998), have resulted in a dramatic lengthening of the time that older people and their adult children are ageing together.

A significant consequence of this is that both generations can expect to go through together many life transitions and milestones not experienced by previous cohorts (Lowenstein, 2007), or what Hagestad and Herlofsen (2007) refer to as 'joint survival, durable ties'. However, the way in which these are experienced and acted out by families are extremely diverse, sometimes uncertain and, given that they are subject to both continuity and discontinuity, cannot easily be reduced to generalisations. We can draw on a number of recognisable familial/ intergenerational 'types': 'tight knit', 'sociable', 'obligatory', 'intimate but distant' and 'detached' (Connidis, 2001: 126) and we can rate them according to affinity, opportunity, functional exchange and so on, but such descriptors tell us little about the qualitative experience of older parent–adult child relationships as they age together and continue to 'do family'. Each relationship 'type' will be mediated by familial, individual and socially constructed biographies and played out within a particular cultural context in a diversity of family practices.

This chapter seeks to explore some of the tensions, contradictions and apparent ambiguities that underpin the ways in which older parents and adult children construct and manage their relationships as they age together. We take the view that such relationships are often ambivalent (Luscher, 2002) – comprising as they do mixed feelings and contradicting expectations – but that most families cope with these ambiguities in a variety of ways. Indeed, some commentators have suggested that the mediation of these intergenerational tensions is in itself an expression of solidarity within families (Lowenstein, 2007). Specifically, we seek to make explicit those issues that pertain to intergenerational family practices as older people now in their late 70s and older, and their ageing adult children, continue to practise family life. Whilst our discussion focuses on that particular intergenerational relationship, we do of course recognise that family relationships are multigenerational and diverse, and that one relationship does not operate in isolation from others. Therefore many of the issues raised in this chapter will be further developed in subsequent chapters. The chapter employs a lifecourse perspective by arguing that these relationships take place within a shared (individual and collective) biography of family practices and ways of 'doing family' (Morgan, 1996). The diversity and complexity of older parent–adult child relationships and the embeddedness of such in family practices will be considered. Wherever possible, the voices of older people and/or their adult children will be used to illustrate the discussion.

Continuity and discontinuity

Relationships between parents and children are subject to both continuity and change throughout the lifecourse, and families in later life are no exception to this. As well as the inevitable change resulting from the family lifecycle, partnering and re-partnering, formation of new families, creation of new generations, death of partners and so on (see Chapters Five, Six and Seven), many of the changes in later life are brought about by what has been termed the 'dualities' of ageing itself (see Godfrey et al, 2004). Such a perspective conceptualises old age as a dual process in which there is both loss and/or adjustment alongside opportunity. These changes are managed, consciously and unconsciously, through processes such as selection, compensation and optimisations (see for example, Baltes and Baltes, 1990) but we argue that they do not operate in a vacuum. Instead, the changes take place within the continuity of family practices, which Hockey and James contend is:

a repertoire of roles and relationships which resources the interpersonal negotiations of individuals whose embodied relationships with one another are both traced through the biological connections of 'blood' and 'genes' as well as being lived out in the every day materially grounded activities of eating and sleeping ... (Hockey and James, 2003: 176–7)

Thus the tensions and ambiguities brought about by 'discontinuity' are mediated and played out within these family practices. Notions 'of' family and 'doing family' continue between older parents and their adult children, even when the balances of losses over gains (resulting from ageing) become increasingly more difficult. As a result of this it is likely that, as Matthews (2002) reminds us, there will increasingly be a blurring of lines between traditional interactions (doing with) and care-giving interactions (doing for), but we argue that family practices remain the bedrock of these interactions.

A number of factors, inherent in individual (and shared) biography and social location, may have different effects on how older parent and adult child interactions are negotiated as parents grow older. Lifelong 'gendered practices' (Morgan, 1996: 11), for example, may overlap with family practices in shaping the way in which different family tensions are managed or at least explained. Most commentators, and indeed older families themselves, accept the closeness of mother–daughter relationships over the lifecourse and the potential for such bonds to become stronger with age (Silverstein and Bengtson, in Connidis, 2001: 124). Cohort expectations may also shape such expectations and assumptions (Chambers, 2005).

In some families, where there are female and male children, lifelong partiality towards certain children on the basis of gender may continue to be a cause of resentment and tension, albeit one that has to be managed. A sister with two brothers explained: 'I was very angry about my mother giving him the money but she always showed partiality towards her sons. I was just a girl. They had all the brains. She had really no respect for me since she felt girls weren't equal to boys' (Matthews, 2002: 91). What might be perceived as preferential treatment may of course also occur in relation to particular adult children regardless of gender. For example, an 83-year-old female participant in Chambers' (2006) study of sibling relationships in later life commented in relation to her sister: 'She was always mother's favourite even when we all got older, it caused such friction.'

Change can, of course, occur on a number of different fronts, some of which we explore in more detail in later chapters, changes resulting from: births and deaths, re-partnering, arrival of in-laws, health status, finances, employment and retirement and so on. However, let us here consider moving house as an example of change. Although many older parents have at least one adult child (or other relative) living relatively close (Cabinet Office, 2008), this is not the case for everyone. As we discuss in Chapter Eight, many older families seek to balance both continuity and change when managing family life 'at a distance'. Sometimes, though, the qualitative impact of adult children moving away can affect the nature of family relationships, as indicated by a focus group participant in a study by Godfrey et al (2004: 144): '... and the children have moved away and the link isn't strong enough ... I would like a special place [in their lives] but there isn't the opportunity to do this.' Clare indicates the tension between knowing that she has a son who continues to care about her and the discontinuity brought about by his move to Australia:

> My son's in Australia and he's wonderful, I would only have to ring him and he'd come across if I needed ... he told me when my husband went off, mum you never worry again ... and he does mean that, he does ... but he is in Australia. (in Shardlow et al, 2008)

Making sense of, negotiating and maintaining family life within the context of continuities and discontinuities brought about by the ageing of all parties, as well as change resulting from the broader circumstances of shared lives, would seem to involve managing adjustment to differential power relationships and shifting needs while making the most of opportunities as they present themselves. However, as Connidis (2001) reminds us, as with all close ties, those between parents and children typically involve tensions and ambivalence that may lead to conflict or be successfully negotiated.

Agency of individual and agency of others

As adults (in western society) move into old age their capacity for agency is sometimes questioned both at an individual/familial level, perhaps based on concerns for perceived frailty, and also at a structural level via attitudes and processes of ageism; that is, discrimination based on negative attributes related to age (Phillipson, 1998). As with all processes of discrimination, ageism may be internalised or resisted but neither older parents nor their ageing adult children are immune to the social context in which they live. Within a family the strive for agency by an ageing parent may be at odds with the concerns of adult children for their parents' safety and also their own concerns for agency. This takes place within an individual family biography and a lifecourse of managing tensions relating to agency and protection. What is now different from earlier in their collective lifecourse is that both parties are 'ageing adults', managing the transitions of later life together. The potential tension that arises from those differing perspectives will be managed by families in different ways and will be highly dependent on family practices embedded within their own collective lifecourse.

In a study of North American older families, Matthews (2002: 149) uses the term 'active resisters' to describe those older parents who strived, usually successfully, to thwart their children's attempts to restrict their capacity for agency. Often this was based on a lifecourse family role, for example: 'Mother is the decision-maker still. As long as she is able, mother is definitely head of the family' (cited in Matthews, 2002: 151). Other older parents used strategies, honed throughout the lifecourse, to maintain agency successfully through active or passive resistance. For example, an adult child who thought her/his mother should visit her doctor offers the flowing explanation: 'I told her we'd get her to the doctor. Before we left she promised she would but she hasn't gone to this day. She'll "yes" you to death but she'll do what she wants to do. She's a real stubborn person' (cited in Matthews, 2002: 154–5).

Yet other older parents maintained agency by employing what may have been lifelong ways of doing family, and indeed parenting, by making choices about what information to divulge to their adult children and what to keep to themselves. Matthews (2002: 157) comments that in families in which children were antagonistic towards, jealous of or competitive with one another, some parents may have been very careful with information to avoid causing additional strain. Interestingly, adult children reported a variety of responses to older parents' resistance to perceived loss of agency, ranging from attempts to challenge evidence of parental control through subterfuge to acceptance and/or pride mixed with anxiety: 'The siblings ... and particularly the sisters, given their propensity to monitor, were not always pleased with their parents' decisions; but on the whole they accepted them even when the consequences were extremely inconvenient or worrisome for them' (Matthews, 2002: 163).

What is evident in this study is that there are both inherent tensions, and a desire for resolution or maintenance of balance by adult children, and perhaps to a lesser extent their older parents, when it comes to managing often competing demands for agency. This frequently involves complex negotiations that take account of family practices over the lifecourse. Furthermore, there is a diversity of experience resulting from those negotiations. A UK study of ageing confirms this complexity and the desire for resolution of potential conflict:

> ... our study revealed a rich pattern of reciprocity and mutual exchange, with active older people playing a significant part as givers of help. As people became more limited by ill-health or advanced old age, the flow of exchange shifted. Even so, acceptance of help from close family members was subject to complex negotiations and characterised by efforts to maintain balance. (Godfrey et al, 2004: 167)

The problem with 'autonomy'

Older people themselves report 'inner' tensions and contradictions in relation to the relationship they have with their sons and daughters and the way in which they negotiate their lives together. These feelings are both complex and diverse and influenced by past relationships, family routines and practices and located in a cultural and social context.

For those older people for whom independence is perceived as 'the gold standard' that is to be achieved at all costs, there is often a tension between wanting the autonomy to lead their own lives and wanting their children to lead their own lives, but simultaneously not wanting to feel 'very much on the fringe' (participant in Godfrey et al, 2004: 144) of their children's lives. Laura (in Shardlow et al, 2008) reflected this tension: '[T]hey [the children] all live all over the country and I travel to them, because you know they've all got families and ... they've got their own lives and you've got to let them go, but I can feel a bit neglected sometimes.'

By contrast, and in line with the diversity of relationships that we explore throughout this book, Connidis (2001) suggests that some older people actively employ a more hands-off approach to parenting and thus are very happy to be 'on the fringe'. For example: 'My responsibility is to be there should the children need me ... you know just to be in the background. To be sort of an anchor. That is all. Not to be "in" their lives ... just to be on the peripheral edges' (Goodman and Rubenstein, in Connidis, 2001: 124).

Some of the women in Chambers' (2005) study of later-life widowhood talked about how they used pretence or silence as a protective strategy in communications with adult sons by suggesting they were more autonomous than they actually felt. When recounting telephone conversations with one of her sons, Dorothy (in Chambers, 2005: 197) said (in response to 'How are you?'): 'I used to say "not so good". But he would say, "That's what you always say". So now I say "I'm fine", even if I'm not. But we don't speak that often now.' Dorothy also suggested that this was in line with the way in which she and her husband had behaved towards each other, and thus was a continuation of previous ways of behaving, particularly where feelings were concerned.

For others there is a tension between wanting the support and love of adult children, and wanting to continue to be important in the lives of older children but not wanting to be perceived as a nuisance. As Norah reported: 'Having a loving supportive family ... it's the most important thing [in having a happy life] ... but I don't want to be a nuisance to anybody that's my worry' (in Shardlow et al, 2008)

Differing perceptions of 'autonomy' and thus 'independence' by both older parents and their adult children can also be sources of tension and irritation, particularly in relation to negotiating mutually acceptable help. This is exemplified in the following discussion between a researcher and Mrs Varley, who is expressing annoyance at her adult, co-resident, son's unilateral decision to replace all the electrical plugs with ones set at a higher level.

> Mrs Varley: Look what my son has done at the weekend. He makes me feel 90. He's put all the plugs on there.
> Q: Is that so it is easier for you?
> Mrs Varley: I can manage them. They were only just on the floor.
> Q: But has he done it to make life easier?
> Mrs Varley: I'd appreciate it more if he did his bedroom.
> Q: Ah bless him, he tried didn't he.

Mrs Varley: Yes but he doesn't try for the things that I want trying.
(in Godfrey et al, 2004: 142)

What is particularly interesting in this example is the way in which differing perceptions – and expressed irritation – of 'what is helpful and for whom' are manifest, and also the way in which the power dynamics of a parent–child relationship are played out between Mrs Varley and her son, suggesting more continuity than discontinuity of family practices.

Clearly, tensions resulting from a range of issues relating to agency, autonomy and dependence will differ from family to family. Nonetheless we argue, with some certainty, that the way in which such perceptions and consequent irritations are managed and experienced will be predicated on how they have always been managed.

Parental identity

In her own way, Mrs Varley is also laying claim to her identity as a mother; indeed her reference to her son's bedroom is reminiscent of parent–adolescent tensions and irritations. There is considerable evidence to suggest that being a parent in old age continues to be an important source of identity for many older people. A 76-year-old widow in Connidis' (2001: 123) study speaks for many older people in her view of 'once a parent, always a parent': 'You never cease being a parent, you know ... I worry about her just as much as I did when she was a child coming home to you.' This might manifest itself in a number of ways. Jerrome's extensive work on the social world of day centres (for example, Jerrome, 1981; 1990) provides many examples of the way in which older women exhibited and reinforced their identity as mothers, for example through conversation about the achievements of adult sons or daughters, sharing photographs or bringing in recent cards and letters to read to other day-centre participants. It is interesting to note that for some of the older women in Jerrome's studies this public display of parental pride and identity, and the picture of family life that they portrayed, was often at odds with the reality of their relationships with their adult children.

Just as there are a variety of family types, there are of course many different ways of parenting; the subsequent relationships that ensue from those diverse parenting styles will also vary considerably. In some families there may be very little change over the lifecourse in the way in which parents and children interact. Some adult children, for example, may continue to resist attempts by their older parents to give what the children perceive as unwelcome advice, make demands on their time and so on. Pat, a widow, aged 66, in Chambers (2005) recognised the tension and irritation inherent in her relationship with her only daughter, who is single and childless, as they grow old together; she reflected that often the arguments they now have are reminiscent of those that took place in the past when her daughter was an adolescent, with neither of them really being prepared to back down. She saw herself as a 'good and caring' mother whereas her daughter perceived her to be a controlling parent. It would seem that old habits, even those relating to parenting, sometimes never die.

Elizabeth, aged 84, by contrast (in Chambers, 2005), while still expressing great pride and joy in her identity as a mother (and grandmother), demonstrated great respect for her daughters and praised their capacity as ageing adults. Together, they tried to maintain as many of their past routines as was deemed possible. For example, at Christmas Elizabeth would prepare cakes, puddings and preserves as she had always done, but increasingly her children provided more input. Family events that had in the past taken place at Elizabeth's house gradually started to be held at the home of one of her daughters, with the proviso that Elizabeth continued to be in charge of arrangements. Both her daughters still sought her advice, often in relation to their own families, and perceived her to be the undeniable head of the family. Maintenance of family routine was also highlighted by Mrs Hyde (in Godfrey et al, 2004: 141) as a way of continuing to be a parent. After recounting how her children (and grandchildren) 'popped in for meals', she said: 'I wouldn't be without them.' Ongoing family routines therefore have the potential to reinforce lifelong ways of being a parent and doing family and thus contribute to the maintenance of identity of the older person and to some extent their children. However, levels of reciprocity, and the capacity for older parents and their children to become companions and/or confidants, as in the example of Elizabeth, will be very dependent on individual and familial biography.

For most older people, then, identity as a parent is a significant feature of later life, with pity often openly expressed for those older people who have never been parents or whose adult children are conspicuous by their absence (Chambers, 2005), even though, as we have explored so far, parenthood in later life is not without complexities and ambivalence. Evidence suggests that the concerns of many older parents remain very similar to those earlier in the lifecourse: concern for their children's well-being and – if they have more than one child – concern for their children to 'get along' (Connidis, 2001; Chambers, 2005). Indeed, the lives of many older people continue to be dominated by doing good for the family. While such practices have the potential to reinforce family solidarity, it is possible that they may also be restrictive.

Biography and family tensions

So far we have argued that most families seem to maintain child–parent ties in later life, relying on family rituals and long-standing ways of doing family: ties of affection, shared biography and a commitment to keeping in touch, either face to face or at a distance, are more likely to enhance the quality of that experience. Ambivalence exists as a feature of family life, but most older families seem to cope with the tensions and ambiguities therein. However, it would be foolhardy to suggest that this is the case for all older parents and adult children. In this final section we explore how for some older families conflict and difference embedded within individual or collective biographies may be so great that family practices cannot be sustained. Previous – perhaps tenuous – ties of affection, or ways of doing family that enabled them to get by earlier in the lifecourse may no longer be present. Anne, for example, in a study of 'loneliness in old age', forcefully expressed her feelings about her unsatisfactory relationship with her family and what she perceives to be a lack of both affection and commitment:

> I have three children who live in another part of the country. But they do not care. Matter of fact they've moved and I don't know where they live ... and I never see my grandchildren, my daughter never lets us see them. My son is rather nasty. (in Shardlow et al, 2008)

Our second example of family conflict in later life is very a different one and comes from research undertaken by one of us. Intergenerational family ties, commitment and affection were for many years the norm for Sylvia (aged 73, in Chambers, 2005). She talked warmly about her own mother, who had provided her and then her baby with unstinting support and affection when she became pregnant as a teenager. When she married, 12 months after her daughter's birth, the relationship between the two women became even stronger. Her new husband adopted her daughter and they went on to have a son. Sylvia in her turn supported her mother, who was subsequently widowed and came to live with Sylvia, her husband and children in what became a fully functioning multigenerational household with its own rituals and family practices. Indeed, she cared for her mother when she became ill and until she died.

Sylvia had always assumed that she and her children, their partners and grandchildren would have a similar relationship and would continue their own ways of doing family. In widowhood, however, there was a falling out when Sylvia met a new partner, whom her daughter could not accept. This was then further aggravated, irrevocably as it turned out, by the inadvertent revelation by a neighbour of a what had been a long-held family secret regarding her daughter's biological father. Sylvia's daughter then severed all links with her family, feeling that they had deceived her. Sylvia has made a new life for herself with her new partner, has strong ties with her son, daughter-in-law and grandson but continues to grieve for the loss of her daughter and grandchildren, and what she thought would be a lifelong relationship and continuation of her own family practices. Her experience demonstrates the way in which major family conflict, deeply embedded in individual and family biographies, can still occur late in life and be irreconcilable.

Over 30 years ago, Johnson (1978) reminded us of the importance of the past for better understanding the present; his comments are particularly pertinent when we are considering the current relationships between some older people and their adult children, which may be rooted in past conflict, a negative experience of family practices or – as we saw in the example above – in family secrets. Ageing, and particularly the potential discontinuities brought about by the ageing process, ill-health, disability, retirement and widow(er)hood, may serve to compound these difficulties.

This is certainly the case in our final example: Marion (in Shardlow et al, 2008), for whom past tensions, power struggles and ways of doing family are now exacerbated by changes brought about by ageing. She describes how the difficulties resulting from her increasing visual impairment have exacerbated what were already strained family ties:

> Being invisible and excluded I can't fight back, I'm left out all over the place. It makes me feel resentful that I am forgotten. They do this for a lot of mature people, don't they ... they leave them out of the conversation all together ... I feel most vulnerable when I go to me daughters, I feel like a prisoner. They just leave me to stew in my own juice. I just want to feel part of the action ... I don't like going. I'd rather stay here and be miserable on my own ...

Marion's comment: 'They do this for a lot of mature people, don't they?' is a stark reminder that, as we discussed earlier, personal and family biography is also located within in a wider cultural context in which structural oppression and ageist attitudes persist.

Conclusion

What is clear from the preceding discussion is the diversity of experience within families and the way in which that experience is subject to both continuity and change: continuity inherent in the family lifecourse and the practices embedded therein; change resulting from individual, family or social circumstances and the processes of ageing itself. Some of the tensions and ambiguities of family relationships have been considered, and we have argued for a biographical approach to improve understanding of the complexities of ageing families. Parent–child relationships continue to be both bounded and of great significance as both parties age together. As we discuss in subsequent chapters, though, such relationships are not exclusive of other relationships. Many older people are enmeshed in a variety of diverse family and non-kin relationships that are also subject to both change and discontinuity and are themselves embedded in biography and family practices. Equally, parent–child practices are not immune to the context in which they operate, whether that be at a macro level, the society in which they are located, their structural location within that society, and the policies and laws that regulate that society; or at a micro level, the local community in which the activity of doing family takes place.

Note

[1] We use the generic term 'adult children', whilst recognising that it is not always clear in the literature whether this refers to birth children, stepchildren or adopted children. It may in some cases include in-laws. According to Matthews (2002), the extent to which an in-law is considered as 'one of the children' and thus incorporated into the older parent–adult child relationships will be dependent on a number of factors. These include: shared biography, congruence/incongruence with their own family of origin and whether their own parents are still alive.

FOUR

Long-lasting relationships

Introduction

Long-lasting heterosexual marriage is only one manifestation of a diverse range of intimate relationships now occurring in later life. As discussed more fully in Chapter One, the relationships that ageing adults construct are increasingly likely to reflect more fluid forms of attachment that challenge traditional notions of family life. As Huyck (2001) specifies, these include remarriage, cohabitation, living apart together, affairs and absent relationships. Moreover, divorce is increasingly common among those people married for two, three or more decades, a trend that is set to continue (Arber et al, 2003). Consequently, a higher proportion of older adults are likely to experience more than one marriage across the lifecourse, or indeed have a combination of relationship forms, which may or may not include marriage. In the context of these more varied and flexible forms of family practice, negotiating relationships is likely to be undertaken in a more reflexive manner, responding to individualised circumstances and contexts, rather than tightly prescribed traditional frames of reference.

Currently, however, marriage remains the dominant form of heterosexual partnership, especially for those in later old age who have remained in long-term relationships (Askham et al, 2007). Indeed, for men and women who were courting and making decisions to marry in the post-Second World War period, marriage was the only form of committed union accorded legitimacy. In an era that has been described as aggressively heterosexual, marriage conferred authority and supremacy on an exclusive sexual relationship between one man and one woman, making all other forms of intimacy appear, at best, inferior and, at worst, deviant (Holden, 2007). Moreover, while there was greater emphasis placed on the notion of 'companionate marriage' than in the first half of the 20th century, this did not reflect an aspiration of equality between spouses. Rather, as Finch and Summerfield (1991: 30) comment, cultural expectations invoked a highly gendered division of labour, with women as wives who 'were to be more comradely, and might be permitted to have outside interests, but were also to be better mothers of larger families, better sexual partners and better home makers'.

Conversely, the cultural context that informed non-heterosexual older men's and women's experiences of relationship formation at this time was fundamentally influenced by powerful anti-homosexual sentiment. Not only was male homosexuality illegal in Britain until 1967, but equally political and religious organisations were instrumental in characterising same-sex relationships as deviant, anti-Christian and a danger to heterosexual marriage and family life (Rosenfeld, 1999; Porche and Purvin, 2008). The prestigious American Psychological Association continued to define homosexuality as a mental disorder until as late as 1973. For a non-heterosexual adult, acknowledging one's sexuality may have fundamentally ruptured family relationships. In the circumstances, men and women often hid their sexual identities, instead 'passing' as heterosexual, some to the extent of marrying (Rosenfeld, 1999). The history of discrimination and oppression experienced by non-heterosexual older people at this time led to relationships being less visible, in what Porche and Purvin (2008) describe as a 'don't ask – don't tell' response to a climate of intolerance.

With this as background, the aim of this chapter is to explore how long-lasting intimate relationships are organised and experienced in the context of ageing. Using relevant literature, the chapter examines three main features of long-term relationships: established divisions of labour, relationship maintenance and the impact of retirement. Where appropriate, the arguments made are illustrated with narrative extracts taken from indepth biographical interviews conducted with heterosexual couples married for 35 years or more. These interviews, conducted as part of a separate study, explored continuity and change in the context of long-lasting marriage relationships and emerging illness (Ray, 2000; 2006).

Before turning to consider these three issues, it is worth highlighting the limited research there has been on long-term relationships in later-life. Undoubtedly research on long-lasting heterosexual marriage has achieved far greater visibility than research on non-heterosexual relationships. But that said, the focus has generally been concerned with identifying factors that contribute to 'satisfaction' in marriages or that emphasise informal care arrangements for older disabled people (Ray, 2000). Studies that seek to illuminate the ways in which heterosexual couples manage the complexities of their relationship across the lifecourse remain rare, perhaps a further indication of the marginality of older people to mainstream concerns (Askham, 1995). A recent systematic analysis of research exploring late-life marriage has concluded that there is an urgent need to explore a much wider research agenda, including, for example, the dynamics of relationships in the absence of ill-health, the strengths of marriage relationships and the effect of wider social contexts on marriages (Walker and Luszcz, 2009). In comparison, though, non-heterosexual relationships are much more seriously under-researched. Indeed, until relatively recently, non-heterosexual relationships among older people constituted 'the most invisible of an already invisible minority' (Blando, 2001: 87).

It is worth recognising that older non-heterosexual men and women are particularly likely to live alone (de Vries, 2007). One survey of older gay, lesbian, bisexual and transsexual (GLBT) men and women living in New York found that 65% of the surveyed population reported living alone, nearly twice the rate of heterosexual older men and women (Cahill et al, 2000). However, de Vries (2007: 21) has commented that analysis is frequently based on assumptions that couples must necessarily share a residence and is 'perhaps part of a hetero-normative and traditional bias that pervades this literature and our thinking on couples and families'. Critically, non-heterosexual relationships among older men and women are likely to include a diverse range of relationship forms, not all of which will involve shared residency. Whatever the form taken, research with non-heterosexual older men and women has highlighted the value placed on couple relationships and the benefit and value of sustained relationships in later life (eg Heaphy et al, 2004; Porche and Purvin, 2008).

Organising divisions of labour

The domestic and intimate lives of long-lasting married heterosexual couples are routinely based on traditionally gendered norms. These relationships are marked by structural inequalities with regard to labour, access to economic resources, status and power. In contrast, the limited research relating to same-sex partnerships suggests a fundamental difference between heterosexual and non-heterosexual intimate relationships. It is argued that same-sex couples can remain relatively free of feminine and masculine stereotypes. Given the absence of prescriptive guidelines reinforced by a long tradition of gender inequality, non-heterosexual couples have the potential to develop relationships based on principles of egalitarianism, independence and agency (Heaphy et al, 2004).

For many women who married during the years following the Second World War, paid employment was neither an accepted nor an acceptable part of married life. Invariably, women were required to give up paid employment when they married:

> Until I was married, yes, I enjoyed my work. I wasn't allowed to work after I was married as they didn't employ married women in the office. (Mrs L, aged 84, in Ray, 2000: 175)

> She had a marvellous job. She was a Company Secretary when I met her and she was earning a lot more than I was. But in those days, policemen's wives weren't allowed to work and things were very strict in those days. (Mr E, aged 85, in Ray, 2000: 175)

Limited years of work, unequal pay and conditions and the cessation of employment upon marriage set the scene for a lifecourse influenced by structural disadvantage and forced reliance on a husband's ability to finance the domestic unit. As Mason (1987) has commented, it rested upon women's shoulders to ensure effective management of the finances, however meagre they may have been.

Upon marriage, women entered a tightly prescribed and highly gendered division of labour characterised by masculine hegemony based on the assumption that men worked outside the home and were responsible for the economic resources of the household unit and that women were responsible for domestic provision, care giving, child rearing and servicing the domestic unit. In the two extracts that follow, Mr D and Mr F reflect on the fundamental roles that their wives played in enabling them to work long hours and pursue a career, safe in the knowledge that their domestic lives were well managed by their wives. In many ways, their wives also contributed to and participated in ensuring their husbands' career development:

> Well in the early days C looked after all the money and all the inside and all the housework and what not because I used to work hard ... Anyway, being in the workshop was working all hours ... many a time I've worked 80 or 100 hours a week so she looked after things and when I was home, I endeavoured to look after the outside. (Mr D, aged 81, in Ray, 2000: 179)

> You see we were part of the ... Service and the wife was supposed to be part of the thing. She has to work very hard because all sorts of things had to be done, not least the entertaining which she did very well. She belonged to various associations. This was all part of the ground rules if you like, so she had to work ... in the Red Cross or what have you. E was a member of Farms and Gardens which is the equivalent of the Women's Institute here. (Mr F, aged 92, in Ray, 2000: 176)

Later, it became more acceptable for women to engage in paid work, providing it did not interfere with domestic life and child rearing (Finch and Summerfield, 1991). From their research with married women, Bird and West (1987) suggest that marital responsibilities were as significant as having children in informing the decision to re-enter employment. Married women who wanted to return to paid work in the 1950s had to demonstrate that it would not affect the organisation of family life, as well as convince their husbands that their employment was not a reflection on his ability to provide for the family (Alford-Cooper, 1998). Married women who took on paid work were consequently often engaged in part-time or temporary work that was less secure, less well paid and below their skill level, but which fitted in with their domestic and caring responsibilities (Bird and West, 1987).

   In the following extract, Mrs S, who married in the early 1960s, reflects the tension of balancing the conflicted position of marriage, parenting and domestic responsibility with returning to employment. Her perception is that her husband judged her to be 'too involved' in her work, with the implication that it affected the degree of support she was able to provide for him:

> I think that he probably thought I was too involved in my job at ... um though he was anxious for me to do it ... and I was very anxious to sort of keep going and do it properly. I think I did all the um ... I think I probably did all the normal sorts of things in the home, but perhaps I was, I think he probably felt I was less sympathetic to his problems at school, say. (Mrs S, aged 68, in Ray, 2000: 177)

While family practices in relation to managing divisions of labour and child rearing in marriage may have been renegotiated to a degree across the course of these marriages, in the great majority of cases, as Mason (1987) argues, the arrangements set early in the marriage continued to pattern the division of labour and responsibilities throughout its course.

As noted earlier, the division of domestic and household labour tends to be more egalitarian in non-heterosexual relationships, in part because of the absence of gender-based normative expectations. In her assessment of recent research, Patterson (2000) argues that domestic roles and tasks are organised between non-heterosexual partners on the basis of greater flexibility and more interchangeable roles. Decisions about the distribution of tasks and responsibilities are consequently more responsive to individual ability and consideration of each person's circumstances. Equally, as Weeks et al (1999) point out, non-heterosexual relationships grounded in aspirations of equality and independence are far more likely to approach issues of domestic organisation as ones requiring discussion, negotiation and agreement.

Other research has argued that, while non-heterosexual couples may claim to operate from a basis of egalitarianism, the division of labour can still be quite marked. For example, Carrington (1999) points to the effect that different forms of employment can have. Age has also been identified as a factor associated with more rigid role divisions, particularly in respect of non-heterosexual males. Previous experience of heterosexual marriage prior to being re-partnered in a non-heterosexual relationship also appears to influence the patterns of responsibility assigned in relationships (Heaphy et al, 2004). In turn, Johnson (1990) has argued that many long-lasting lesbian relationships are premised on a commitment to fairness and justice based on an appreciation of individual difference and strengths, rather than a straightforward 'balancing of scales'. The crucial issue here is that while some non-heterosexual couples may engage in behaviours that might seem to reflect traditional roles, they are likely to do so on the basis of choice and negotiation, with decisions routinely open to later renegotiation. A participant in research by Heaphy et al highlights this position:

> I occasionally look and think 'My God! We're a 1950's butch/femme couple' ... I'm reasonably comfortable with that ... as I've got older I've got easier about the fact that I actually do like cooking and I really don't like hammering nails into fences ... because the fact that two adults of the same gender choose to do different things within the house, doesn't give kids a message that says 'Men are only supposed to do this one' or 'Women are only supposed to do that one'. (Heaphy et al, 1999: 234)

Clearly this is different to the patterns developed in most heterosexual marriages.

Making it last: sustaining intimate couple relationships

How are couple relationships sustained as long-lasting, often lifelong, commitments? Although relationship longevity may reduce some of the need for active maintenance strategies, Duck (1999: 77) argues that '[I]t is unlikely that mere longevity of the relationship keeps them going, and it is more probable that something else is necessary, something strategic or active or shared jointly that polishes up the relationship.' Continuity theory (Atchley, 1999) provides some insight into the ways adults may achieve relationship continuity based on successful adaptation to change and transition over the course of the relationship. Successful adaptation is likely to lead to greater confidence in the relationship and the management strategies used to keep it going. However, as we discuss more fully below, unhappy relationships may also be sustained over time, successfully achieving key goals, such as parenting, through the family practices developed. A significant amount of research has tried to isolate the elements that constitute a satisfying long-lasting relationship. This research, most of it based in North America, has focused predominantly on heterosexual marriage, but more recently relationship satisfaction amongst non-heterosexual couples has also been studied.

The research exploring satisfaction in long-lasting marriage has concluded, perhaps not surprisingly, that continuing to like one's marriage partner, demonstrating commitment and fidelity, sharing values and having effective and intimate communication strategies are all key elements of marital satisfaction (Lauer and Lauer, 1990; Kaslow and Robison, 1996). As might be expected, the findings of 'satisfaction research' on same-sex relationships overlap considerably with the results of studies of heterosexual couples. Factors such as positive interaction, mutual affection and enjoyment of the other, and effective communication strategies are all key influences on relationship maintenance (eg Kurdek, 1994, 1995). A qualitative study exploring communication and interaction between non-heterosexual and heterosexual older couples concluded that containment of major conflict and sustaining psychologically intimate communication played a substantial role in shaping satisfaction in lasting relationships, irrespective of sexuality (Mackey et al, 2004).

While satisfaction research indicates key aspects of long-term relationships, it does not always capture the complexity of relationships or how they are managed through the variety of transitions experienced across the lifecourse. As Duck (1999: 73) has commented: 'Relationships are such complex entities that they contain good and bad, rough and smooth, sickness and health, richness and poverty. Thus it is not surprising that people find it to be a variable experience to have relationships, experiencing at different times, a rough ride or a smooth one.'

To understand how relationships are sustained, it is important to explore the meanings that partners ascribe to their relationship experiences and the ways they define and construct their relationships. Biographical interviews with heterosexual couples married for 35 years and longer highlighted the importance of being able to predict with some confidence what their partner's views would be and how they might react to different situations (Ray, 2000). The respondents felt that over time they had built up detailed familiarity and knowledge about their partners through their shared experiences of family life: '... getting close to each other and really getting to know each other ... really so you know, not exactly, but near enough what the other is thinking, and how the other will react, I think that's it' (Mr C, aged 81, in Ray, 2000: 188).

Couples who saw their relationships as emotionally close and generally happy – often characterised as conflict-free – underlined the successful management of the various transitions and problematic events they had experienced over the course of their married lives. They had developed shared narratives characterised by, for example, intimate language (nicknames, shared jokes) and the use of a form of spoken shorthand (Duck, 1999). They drew on anniversaries and other milestones as relationship markers and used reminiscences to reinforce and represent a shared past. For example, couples talked about and gave examples from their marriage biographies of: 'always being there for each other when it was needed', 'facing things head on', 'working together to solve problems' and 'never going to bed on an argument'. They also highlighted the importance of 'singing from the same song book' when managing routine and more significant lifecourse events. For them, this meant having aspirations or goals that were not in conflict, so that differences of opinion and clashes of perspective were minimised. This approach appeared to reflect perceived behavioural 'standards' that had been important across their marriage, as well as a desire to communicate a public story that validated a successful relationship.

Agreement about financial management was also seen as significant by many of the couples, though their money management ideologies and practices varied. A number of the couples highlighted the importance of living within one's financial means and avoiding debt: 'As long as neither of us ever owed any money except the ordinary bills and that, everything was nice and dandy' (Mrs D, aged 86, in (Ray, 2000: 188). Mr and Mrs F (aged 93 and 93) bought their first house with a mortgage, but paid for their later houses outright (Ray, 2000: 188). Similarly Mr G (aged 84) praised his wife because '.... she paid of the mortgage early and systematically' (Ray, 2000: 187). These narratives were used as evidence of a marriage relationship that valued planning, organisation and risk minimisation. Other couples took a rather different view: 'We don't worry about money, as long as we got some money to put in our purse that's all that's important' (Mr and Mrs C. aged 81 and 79, in Ray, 2000: 188). This sort of position was again used as a relationship marker, characterising what couples wished to portray as a more spontaneous, less structured approach to married life. What seems critical to these stories is that the couple essentially agree, or at least do not publicly disagree, with the message that they communicate about their marriages and the practices they entail.

Whilst minimal conflict may contribute to marital continuity, it does not guarantee marital happiness. Nor does a decline in happiness necessarily lead to a decline in commitment. Research suggests that remaining unhappily married is associated with lower levels of overall well-being, self-esteem and higher levels of psychological distress (Hawkins and Booth, 2005). Nevertheless, moral pressure, financial constraints and structural disadvantage may all exert significant pressure on a couple to remain together in an unhappy or devitalised marriage. Marriages may keep going and cope with long-standing, unresolved tensions by 'leaving well alone' (Gottman, 1994) and staying in neutral territory to avoid an escalation of conflict. Couples may adjust by leading relatively separate or parallel lives, coming together when required to do so by duty or when presenting an image of togetherness and family solidarity is important, for example, attending family weddings.

Conflict may therefore remain relatively untouched and unresolved, contributing to ambivalent relationships and having significant implications when, for example, the balance of power shifts between the couple. During her interview, Mrs H (aged 85) reflected on a difficult event she experienced that led to a significant breach of trust early in her marriage. In this extract, she expresses the dismay she felt at her husband's behaviour in the light of her role as domestic provider, mother of two small children and supporter of her husband:

> He worked at D's ... He got friendly with a girl there and I haven't really deep down forgiven him. He didn't go off with her or anything like that but a man at the local shop told me and that did upset us for a bit ... I faced him with it and told him to choose. He's not as strong as I am and I think he got beguiled ... I was very, very hurt. He had to be there for one shift at 6 am and I used to get up at 4.30 and cook him bacon and egg and look after him. The women at D were shocked too and said I must have been a good wife because of H's shirts. (Ray, 2000: 183)

Mrs H's portrayal of herself as 'strong' and Mr H as 'weak' was a theme of this interview. Mrs H.'s analysis persisted into her situation at the time of the interview, when she expressed herself as 'duty bound' to provide care for her disabled husband who made matters worse by not making an effort and 'as ever, taking the line of least resistance'. When she found herself in the situation of becoming his carer, Mrs H's long-standing ambivalence about her relationship, and the difficulties she had in effecting change in her husband's behaviour, spilled over into anger and frustration.

As already noted, the absence of stereotypical feminine/masculine conventions and guidelines in same-sex couples suggests that there are greater possibilities for creating relationships based on egalitarianism (Weeks et al, 1999). In her work, Dunne (1997) has suggested that while traditionally gendered heterosexual couples may be characterised as 'intimate strangers', couples in same-sex relationships can be more accurately portrayed as 'intimate friends'. Certainly much research on long-lasting non-heterosexual relationships, both lesbian and gay, has highlighted the significance of friendship principles in shaping and sustaining these ties (Johnson, 1990; Heaphy et al, 1999; Budgeon, 2006). Such a focus on egalitarianism and friendship in non-heterosexual relationships fosters an awareness of relationship differences (for example, inequalities in income, social class and/or social capital) and, importantly, a greater willingness to discuss and negotiate appropriate resolutions to them (Heaphy et al, 2004).

Given the socio-historical context in which non-heterosexual relationships have evolved, relationship maintenance is likely to include behaviours for dealing with the stresses and challenges associated with discrimination and stigma, including rejection by family. Constructing personal networks of others who are accepting and supportive is likely to be significant in this. More specifically, creating 'families of choice' (Weston, 1991) comprising friends, lovers, co-parents, adopted children, children from previous heterosexual relationships and offspring conceived through alternative insemination contributes to an environment in which different modes of intimate relationship can be sustained. In their study of older non-heterosexual men and women, Heaphy et al (2004: 899) suggest that these constructions of family represent 'innovative strategies for living outside the normative framework … to the extent that some theorists have argued that non-heterosexual lifestyles are the prime experiments in late-modern ways of living'.

For heterosexual couples who met in the 1950s and 1960s, marriage was a key symbol of commitment. There were no socially legitimate alternatives for developing a shared life. In consequence, for heterosexual couples a long-lasting relationship implies a long-lasting marriage. This, of course, is not so for non-heterosexual relationships. Indeed, in Britain legal recognition of such ties has only been possible since 2005, when civil registrations were introduced. Since then, many couples have chosen this route to celebrate and publicly endorse their relationships. But equally many have not, seeing no need for legal recognition of their relationship: 'Legally endorsing a relationship does not make it more of one, and outlawing it does not make it less' (Porche and Purvin, 2008: 155). While material issues of pension provision and inheritance can influence this decision, many non-heterosexual couples in established relationships have constructed other ways of recognising and celebrating their commitment. As with other couples, celebrations of different anniversaries, gift-giving, private rituals, the retelling of shared experiences, and the like, all symbolise and help constitute the commitment that exists.

Retirement

Retirement from paid employment is a significant lifecourse transition that can affect marriage relationships in a number of ways. Retirement of one spouse is likely, for example, to result in both spouses having to adjust to changes in role, in the time spent together, and in access to space, privacy and freedom of movement (Alford-Cooper, 1998). Research on the consequences of retirement for marital satisfaction in long-lasting marriage has drawn a number of conclusions, some of which appear contradictory. Broadly speaking, the research suggests that there is a significant continuity in the quality of marital relationships through the transitions of retirement (Atchley, 1992). Marriages that were in trouble prior to retirement are likely to continue to experience difficulties; enforced time together and impingement on each other's space may escalate conflict and make its management more difficult (Myers and Booth, 1996; Alford-Cooper, 1998). Conversely, couples whose marriages are successful and happy are more likely to report an increase in marital closeness following retirement (Kulik, 2000). The transitions to retirement that are most likely to create tension within a marriage include: being reluctant to retire or being forced into retirement with little preparation (Barnes and Parry, 2004); wives choosing to remain at work when their husbands have retired, especially if their husbands continue to perceive themselves as the primary wage earner/breadwinner (Szinovacz and Schaffer, 2000); and wives who are reluctant to retire but feel that they must do so at the same time as their husbands (Szinovacz, 1991).

Research has emphasised the importance in retirement of preserving existing activities and friendships, as well as developing new ones. Some gender differences are apparent in this. In particular, men who have relied on workplace contacts for sociability may find developing new friendships in retirement difficult, and yet they no longer have occasion to maintain their previous ties. Indeed, men frequently rely most heavily on their partners and immediate family for emotional support. They can as a consequence experience considerable isolation if they subsequently lose the support of their spouse through death (Jerrome and Wenger, 1999; see Chapter Seven).

Some research has suggested that divisions of household labour become more equitably distributed following retirement, with older men taking more responsibility for domestic work than they had prior to retirement (Szinovacz, 2000). Other research on long-married couples, however, suggests that divisions of labour remain essentially unchanged, with male participation in household work most often remaining at the level of superficial involvement (Ray, 2000). Mason (1987), in a groundbreaking qualitative study, concluded that a fundamental renegotiation of gendered responsibilities is unlikely to occur in later life. More typically, retired husbands tend to encroach on women's domestic territory, causing wives to feel that they do not have the same freedom to organise their lives as they had before their husbands' retirement.

Moreover, Mason's analysis demonstrated that men and women had a strong investment in their traditional divisions of labour. Whilst husbands may provide some assistance in the domestic sphere, that assistance was often characterised in terms of an 'incompetent husband' assisting the 'expert wife'. Thus wives maintained their control and authority in the domestic arena. Mason (1987: 102) extends this argument into an analysis that proposes that: 'Through the payment of lipservice to women's domestic power, the ultimate "orchestration" power of husbands over their wives, stemming from their socially advantaged position, can be concealed whilst also being reinforced.' Mason's analysis offers an explanation that links divisions of labour with the continuing distribution of power between men and women who have sustained traditionally gendered roles through the course of their marriage.

In comparison to heterosexual couples, there is a dearth of research on the effect of retirement for non-heterosexual partnerships. The research that does exist tends to focus on the policy and legislative changes required to address the consequences of the discrimination that non-heterosexual people have experienced across the lifecourse (Cahill and South, 2002).

One way in which aspirations for retirement may become compromised is through the experience of illness by one or both partners. Arber and Ginn (1991) analyse the extent to which both older men and women provide informal support for their long-term ill or disabled partners. In long-term marriages, support for an ill spouse clearly occurs within the context of a developed relationship, yet research that focuses on the perspectives of both partners in the relationship is rare (Parker, 1993; Twigg and Atkin, 1994). It would be useful to develop clearer understandings of how couples' different relational biographies influence their experience of giving and receiving care and how this latter, in turn, affects their relationship.

Narrative research exploring the ways in which spousal support is provided for an ill partner suggests considerable diversity in how caring roles are constructed (Ray, 2000). In cases where both partners experience ill-health, couples may define themselves as interdependent, providing mutual support and assistance to each other. Over time, caring activities may fluctuate, cease or even be swapped between the partners in response to their changing health needs. Interestingly, what is defined as 'care' by spouses may vary along gender lines. Husbands are likely to perceive domestic work as caring, whereas wives see domestic work as part of their usual activities and reserve the label 'caring' for personal, intimate and supervisory tasks.

There has been little research exploring how illness and disability is managed in the context of long-lasting non-heterosexual relationships. What there is identifies the importance of a partner as a key support in the event of illness (Heaphy et al, 2004). It also points to a lack of trust in formal services among older non-heterosexual men and women. In particular, formal services dominated by heterosexual assumptions or predicated around beliefs about the asexuality of older people are unlikely to provide appropriate and sensitive support to gay and lesbian older couples facing illness or disability. Older non-heterosexual men and women may have spent their adult lives making complex decisions and choices about whether or not, when and to whom they reveal their sexuality. Price (2008: 1344), reflecting on the experience of dementia for non-heterosexual older people, observes that a diagnosis of dementia releases a 'minefield of potential "outings"', with what were previously private matters now opened up to public scrutiny. Clearly, there is a need to develop more complete understandings of the ways in which ageing in a non-heterosexual context shapes the experience of providing and receiving care within intimate relationships.

Conclusion

It is likely that heterosexual marriage will continue to be a central relationship among older people. However, long-lasting marriage will be only one of the ways in which intimate relationships are expressed and sustained in older age. The range of committed relationships that people may experience through the lifecourse will be reflected in increasingly diverse and fluid family practices, among older as well as younger cohorts. There is a need for research to capture this diversity in older people's intimate ties more fully. For example, how childless long-term married couples – whether childless through choice or circumstance – experience old age remains substantially unexplored (Dykstra, 2006; Dykstra and Hagestad, 2007). Similarly, the partnership experiences of older people from minority ethnic groups with their own distinct family practices have been under-researched. Older non-heterosexual men and women have recently begun to be more visible in research but our knowledge of the issues and dilemmas faced by those in long-term partnerships remains very limited. This is an important gap given the changes there have been in gay and lesbian lifestyles in recent years. Indeed, all these and other areas of 'new' partnership behaviour warrant fuller research attention.

FIVE

Brothers and sisters

Introduction

This chapter explores the way in which brothers and sisters grow up and grow old, together and apart. Specifically, it will address the way in which older siblings negotiate continuities, and manage the discontinuities brought about by ageing. The study of siblings in later life is a neglected area, particularly in the UK. A preoccupation with relationships of care and increasing interest in intergenerational support, solidarity and ambivalence has shifted the gerontological gaze from intra-generational ties. And yet, Bengtson's (2001: 6) notion of co-survivorship among generations (see also Chapters One and Three) could equally be applied to intra-generational relationships. Many of the current cohort of older people will as children have experienced the death of siblings early on in life from childhood diseases largely now eradicated, as well as the loss of siblings in adulthood as a result of war, accident or illness. They may not have expected to share a prolonged period of time in later life growing old either together or apart. Yet, for many older people this is exactly what has happened: the likelihood of having a surviving sibling in later life is high (Cicirelli, 1995).

Researching adult sibling relationships is not easy (Mauthner, 2002; Walker et al, 2005); such relationships are diverse, unregulated, complex, ever-changing and methodologically challenging. What, for example, constitutes a sibling: does this include 'step' and 'half' brothers and sisters? Add in 'old age' and the variables become even greater: each sibling relationship in later life will have its own history and will be enmeshed in the lifecourse of an individual, a family, a cohort and the societal context in which each of these occurs. The little research that there is on older siblings suggests that being a brother or sister becomes increasingly important for many older people as they age, with talk about siblings featuring in older people's stories as a valuable component of later life (Gold, 1987; Connidis, 2001; Chambers, 2005). Indeed, Gold (1987: 207) goes so far as to say: '... that the sibling relationship makes a unique and significant contribution to the lives of many older people is a significant conclusion drawn by ... older people themselves and one that family researchers might well heed'.

By comparison with other family relationships, our knowledge of the experience and feelings related to being a sibling in later life is still relatively scarce. We know even less of the effect of such relationships on the overall experience of growing older, and more specifically on the construction of identity in later life. Gold's comment in 1987 still holds true today:

> Conspicuously absent ... are studies of interactions between adult brothers and sisters ... The intensity of feelings about siblings in old age suggests that further study of the later-life sibling bond might increase understanding of ways in which the social and emotional needs of older people can be met. (Gold, 1987: 199)

It is the purpose of this chapter to explore those interactions. Drawing on a small body of relevant literature and recent biographical research with older brothers and sisters, we will explore the way in which current cohorts of older people negotiate sibling relationships and engage in family practices in later life. We will, of course, exercise caution in relation to explanation, evaluation and generalisation, and pay due attention to the complexity and diversity of sibling relationships and the family practices that ensue from those relationships. A lifecourse perspective (Giele and Elder, 1998), grounded in critical gerontology, is employed in which personal/collective biography, ageing, experience and identity are paramount. Where appropriate, the words of older siblings will illustrate the discussion.

Personal and collective biography

Being a sibling is a unique experience, rooted in both personal and collective biography. It is the longest-lasting tie most people will have and brings with it the potential both for shared experience over the lifecourse and for shared reminiscence in later life. Connidis (2001) reminds us that most siblings share commonalities (cultural background, values and genes), but – equally important – there are also many differences, some of which may be reinforced or developed in adulthood (gender, sexual orientation, social mobility and education) and which will inevitably affect (both positively and negatively) family relationships and family practices in later life. Important for the current discussion, siblings have both a shared and a unique narrative of family life; simultaneously there is sameness and difference of experience, perception, memory and identity.

Because a sibling relationship is one of peers, it is essentially egalitarian and thus is the family relationship that most closely parallels friendship. Indeed, some siblings will actually describe their relationship as 'like friends'. By contrast, the expression 'like a sister' is sometimes employed by older women to describe a particularly close friend (Jerrome, 1990; O'Connor, 1992; Chambers, 2005). Adult sibling relationships are simultaneously closer kin and non-kin and comprise a strong element of choice in relation to the particular nature of the relationship. However, unlike friendship, sibling relationships are not voluntary. As Allan (1977) commented, it is possible to have an ex-friend but not an ex-sibling.

In early adulthood, the sibling relationship is essentially one of ambiguity: there are few societal expectations about how to behave, no clearly defined rules, and thus it is open both to interpretation and creativity. Bedford (1989) suggests that the few social expectations that do exist, for example in relation to equity, maturity, loyalty and individuality, are fundamentally contradictory, making sibling ties inherently ambivalent, with harmony and conflict co-existing (cited in Connidis, 2001). While most siblings maintain some sort of contact throughout their lives, there is considerable variation and flexibility of relationships and family practices (Rowe, 2007). Indeed, within families, there is likely to be a diversity of sibling relationships inherent in individual and collective biographies. The following two examples serve to illustrate such diversity. Frances (female, aged 75) for example sought to differentiate between her sibling relationships:

> ... I like being a sister, his sister in particular because he cherishes me ... and E's sister but not C's sister. C and I have never got on. She was father's favourite ... she always saw herself as different from the rest of us, and she still does. E feels the same way about her ... (in Chambers, 2006)

By contrast, May's sibling history reminds us of the complexity of relationships and sibling groupings in large families, not uncommon among the current cohort of older people in the UK. May (female, aged 84) was the second youngest of 10 children. Here she talks about her oldest brother:

> I 'knew about' him but I didn't 'know' him. It felt very strange when I met him for the first time, I was eighteen years old. I saw this big handsome bloke and he was my brother, by this time he was married and had family of his own ... his time in the RAF finished so he came home to find work. I didn't recognise him as my brother, he didn't look like the others, he looked more confident. I never really got to know him ... (in Chambers, 2006)

May was closest to the brother and sister nearest to her in age; indeed, most of her childhood memories relate to these two siblings. Once her brother emigrated with his family to New Zealand, her relationship with him became rather fragmented and, as a result of his death at a relatively young age, did not survive into old age. However her relationship with her sister has endured, with both of them now in their 80s:

> My youngest sister and I never faltered. Of course, we lived together when we [both] first married our husbands were in the army ... Even now it's as close as it has ever been ... we're so alike in many ways. We like to talk about the old days. We reminisce quite a lot and we have a good laugh about some of the things that happened ... sad times as well. And sometimes one of us will remember something that the other one can't remember quite as well and we jog each other's memory a bit. We speak on the phone every night to make sure we are both alright ... We'll keep the relationship going ... It's like it was when we were first married! ... (May, female aged 84, in Chambers, 2006)

The history of relationships with and between in-laws will also affect, both negatively and positively, sibling relationships and has implications for family practices and relationships in old age. Research suggests considerable variability. Drawing on retrospective accounts from older people, Ross and Milgram (1982) reported that although a minority believed marriage had enhanced relationships with siblings, the dominant view was that marriage had impacted negatively on sibling relationships. Chris (male, aged 76, in Chambers, 2006) exemplifies this: 'My attention to my own family [of origin] has always been resented by my wife ... but now I get up and go and do it. My own home would still take priority if there was an event of equal seriousness but my brother and sisters now matter too.' However, research undertaken by Connidis (1994) suggested a more even spread of experience. Indeed, some respondents provided evidence of very strong bonds between in-law siblings. Interestingly, both Chambers (2005) and Martin-Matthews (1991) report examples of older widows who describe their widowed sisters-in-law as 'best friends'.

It is important to remember that these individual relationships exist within wider social structures and thus are not immune to socially constructed norms and practices. For example, in relation to gender: as they age, sisters have been consistently reported (see Von Volkolm, 2006, for a review of the literature) as having a 'special' relationship rooted in their shared gender over the lifecourse (this may as a consequence have heightened the invisibility of relationships and interactions between older brothers); 'oldest' sisters are more likely to play a key role as kin-keepers and maintainers of family practices following the death of parents (Connidis, 2001). They are also extremely important for understanding sibling relationships over the lifecourse; the matrilineal focus among married couples means that married couples are in greater contact with the woman's family, including her siblings (Connidis, 2001). There is also evidence that sibling relationships are culturally constructed. Martin-Matthews (1991), for example, reports that Canadian and Australian research on older widows and their siblings has consistently found evidence for strong emotional bonds with siblings, whereas research in the US suggests that such ties are likely to be with children. Furthermore, White and Riedmann's (1992) research found that African-American adults interacted more with their siblings than those of Caucasian, Mexican-American or Asian-American ethnicity.

Ageing together

The sibling relationship is illustrative of the stability and change inherent in family life (see Chapter One): some ties change over the lifecourse and have to be negotiated and renegotiated but this takes place within taken-for-granted ways of 'doing family'. Gold's typology (Gold, 1989; see also Cicirelli, 1995) identifies five types of sibling relationships: intimate; congenial; loyal; apathetic; hostile (see Table 5.1).

Table 5.1: Sibling typology

Title	Definition
Intimate	High devotion and psychological closeness; based on mutual love, concern, empathy, protection, understanding and durability
Congenial	Strong friendship and caring; less depth and reliability than intimate siblings; regular contact (weekly, monthly)
Loyal	Based on cultural norms rather than personal involvement; support during crises; regular but not frequent contact
Apathetic	Mutual lack of interest in sibling relationship (no emotional or instrumental support); lives gone in different directions and do not care much; minimal contact
Hostile	Strong negative feelings (resentment and anger) towards siblings; considerable negative psychological preoccupation with relationship; no contact

Source: Gold (1989), cited in Cicirelli (1995: 49).

It is probable that the type of sibling relationship experienced in later life is strongly linked to that of the childhood and family relationship – if close bonds and attachments have been forged in childhood it is likely that they will be strong in later life (Burholt and Wenger, 1998) and supportive family practices will be sustained. However, even where siblings have been close, unforeseen family schism can still occur and disrupt such continuities. As we will discuss later, such abrupt discontinuity is likely to have negative consequences for well-being in later life. By contrast, where those ties are not forged (apathetic or hostile), sibling relationships and practices in later life may be less supportive. Patricia (female, aged 67, in Chambers, 2005: 185), for example, described her family of origin as 'nothing to be proud of', citing extreme poverty, a lack of closeness and at times neglect. She described her relationship with her only (younger) sister as 'uneasy' and contended that all that really held them together was duty; her sister wanted to forget their poor childhood and refused to discuss what had happened in the past. As a result of this Patricia felt that her own painful memories of their family life and growing up together were not validated by her sister and she derived little pleasure from her sibling relationship. However, Eunice, a widow of 69 (in Chambers, 2005: 183), described her family of origin as 'very close'. In early adulthood, when marriage, children and work dominated their lives, they had been 'friendly', but in old age her widowed brother had become a significant person in her life and they were now 'much closer'. Indeed, they were now neighbours who shared lunch once a week, taking turns to cook Sunday dinner, as well as enjoying leisure activities together. Eunice enjoyed and valued greatly the relationship they now had.

Most commentators (Bedford, 1989; Connidis and Campbell, 2001; White, 2001) agree that ageing reduces the inherent ambivalence of early adulthood and what might be conceptualised as a maturing or mellowing-out seems to take place in later life. Early adulthood is a time when many siblings form relationships away from the family of origin. Sibling relationships are at this time generally viewed as of lower priority than marital or partner and parent–child relationships; the impact of these changes will of course vary both between and within families. Derek (male, aged 85, in Chambers, 2006), for example, reported: 'We weren't ever enemies but we didn't spend a lot of time with each other and probably the same thing applied when we were married. It's only really been in recent years that we have become close.'

Using data from the Bangor Longitudinal Study on Ageing, Burholt and Wenger (1998) found that although there was evidence of gender-specific differences relating to the closeness of sisters, most sibling relationships became closer in later life. This included those relationships that had previously been problematic. Age differences and rivalries, for example – so pertinent earlier on in the lifecourse – cease to be of such importance for many siblings. Individual experiences of ageing and the lifecourse increase diversity and thus decrease the need to strive for individuality and separateness. Brian (male, aged 69), for example, contrasted his past and present relationship with his brother:

> I looked after my brother because he was my younger brother and I wouldn't let anything happen to him ... I was always told he was my responsibility but he was a pain, there were five years between us ... It was difficult, me dad favoured my younger brother over me and I can never understand this but it caused resentment ... he [brother] lives in Cyprus now and I got a bit of a buzz this last time, when we arrived I heard him shouting so excited and I got a real buzz and when we went out he was telling everyone I was his big brother, it felt so good ... we go each year and in between times we ring each other and send some photos ... (in Chambers, 2006)

For many siblings, then, later life is a time for re-establishing or reaffirming close ties with their family of origin (White, 2001). The drivers would appear to be inherent in the siblings' collective lifecourse, including family practices relating to affection, loyalty and/or duty. Critical and sometimes unhappy incidents, for example the ill-health or death of a family member, or more positive milestones such as special birthdays or anniversaries may provide triggers for siblings to come together and do family. Life-stage events such as retirement or children leaving home to create new families may mean that there is greater time and/or opportunity for siblings to rekindle dormant relationships and family practices. There is also some evidence to suggest that sibling ties are more likely to be strengthened as a result of the divorce or widowhood of a family member (Martin-Matthews, 1991; White, 2001; Chambers, 2005).

Although not the focus of this chapter, it is useful to note that there is some discussion in the literature about support between siblings as they grow older. Siblings are lower in the hierarchy of care relationships and such support is thus very dependent on personal circumstances and personal liking (Finch, 1989). What is clear, however, is that although a sibling relationship does not guarantee assistance, it can nonetheless be very supportive. Siblings tend to keep exchanges equitable, with help likely to be in response to particular situational demands. Indeed, a much stronger notion is that of siblings as sources of 'potential help' (Cicirelli, 1995). Individual and family life histories both have a role in influencing the likelihood of such help being sought and it is important to acknowledge that some individuals make deliberate choices earlier on in their lifecourse to separate themselves from their siblings. For example, one of Mauthner's participants in a study of 'sistering' through the lifecourse (Mauthner, 2002; 2004) had felt rejected by siblings who had been unable to accept her sexuality; instead she chose to reconstruct her family and family practices within the lesbian community where she now lived: it was from that community that she now sought support. Bee (female, aged 68, in Chambers, 2005: 186), by contrast, described her relationship with her own brothers and sisters as: '... mixed. I was one of five children. I seem to have become the most successful of all the children.' There was, she reflected, resentment of her success and she was aware of the huge gulf in social class and lifestyle that had been developing between herself and her siblings since she left home at the age of 18. Widowhood had certainly not brought them any closer; indeed, it had confirmed to Bee that friends were more important than her siblings, with whom she had minimal contact. Despite this negativity towards her siblings, and certainly no expectation of either receiving or giving support, lifelong family practices were nonetheless still evident in the way that she provided financial support for her two nieces. As Connidis reflects:

> On balance, the results concerning sibling support lend support to the view that the same relationship can be negotiated quite differently, depending on an individual's circumstances ... the variability among older persons in the relative significance of siblings as support providers illustrates considerable flexibility in how particular ties are negotiated. (Connidis, 2001: 239)

Being a sibling in later life: a 'special' relationship

There is compelling evidence to suggest that many older people not only value the special relationship they have with siblings but actually exercise agency and choice in order to re-engage with their siblings in later life. For some, the imperative may come from increasing age itself, a feeling that time is running out and along with that the recognition of individual (and collective) mortality: as Chris (male, aged 76), explains:

> As you become elderly, you realise, well you know, that life goes terribly quickly, you are conscious that you haven't got a lot of time left with these sisters and brother ... what brings you even closer is that these other parts of you are very important, they are like a physical part of me and when they go, that's a bit of me that goes. I know that from when my other sister died.... (in Chambers, 2006)

For others, re-engagement with siblings can provide opportunities for reminiscence or life review (see Butler, 1980; Bornat, 1996) and along with that a sense of continuity of experience and self. Even if individual narratives may at times differ within the process of collective reminiscence, such opportunities may offer an opportunity to connect with family of origin. This sense of connectedness may be particularly important when identity is under threat (Matthews 1979; Jenkins, 1996), perhaps because of changes resulting from some of the losses of old age such as ill-health, perceived dependency and loss of autonomy, or from the negative attitudes of significant others and/or more generic experiences of ageism. Many of Chambers' (2006) participants talked about an increasing need for connectedness. For example:

> ... brothers and sisters can talk to each other about the past and about the parents, do you remember this and that, you need someone to follow on after your parents have gone. Its such a help, you've still got a connection, you need connections and your relationships with each other are unique, you can never copy it ... you can have your own family but the family you come from matters. (Female, aged 85, in Chambers, 2006)

> Oh it makes you feel good and you know that that other person, your brother or sister, understands you, what you mean when you try to express your feelings about something that went on in the family, the personal things. They don't see you as an old person, they see you as a brother or sister ... We know what each other likes, that's what makes it so special. (Female, aged 84, in Chambers, 2006)

What is being illustrated here is a mutuality rooted in a collective lifecourse, shared history (Gold, 1987) and family practices, and, as a result, a perception of a more equal relationship in later life with siblings than for example with adult children or for some older people without children, friends. The following two examples serve to illustrate this.

> It's very hard to know how your children see you ... when you get to my age they do sometimes say things or do things that suggest they think you are terribly incompetent but my brothers and sisters don't do that, they've got the picture of me as I used to be when I didn't

need anyone to patronise me ... a more rounded picture of me. (Female, aged 83, in Chambers, 2006)

I can rely on family and I can also rely on my friends ... but if I were ill I would ring W, there is a natural closeness with family, there are times when you don't really need to say much. I suppose you can get that with friends but not to the same degree ... I think it is because of the family bond. With your sister, it's something that's grown with you over time and you can easily plug into it. With friends there is a certain distance, to no detriment, but it's different. It must start off when you are children ... we were together for a long time even up to just before we were married. (Female, without children, aged 85, in Chambers, 2006)

Research demonstrates that those older adults who do have such meaningful contacts with siblings are more likely (than those who do not) to experience life satisfaction, higher morale, fewer depressive symptoms, psychological well-being and a greater sense of emotional security in old age (Bedford, 1997; Connidis and Campbell, 2001). Derek, (male, aged 85) is adamant that his relationship with his brothers contributes to his sense of well-being:

It would never have occurred years ago but now my brothers are an important part of my daily life and how I feel. Without question, this is now an important part of my life, well it's how I feel anyway, I don't know how they would feel but I think both of them would say the same. It's part of my daily routine, the way I manage my time and my life. We talk such a lot now. (in Chambers, 2006)

Interestingly, Cicirelli's (1995) study suggests that simply knowing that a sibling is potentially available is in itself a source of emotional comfort. For some older people, this may in later life be sufficient to help to reduce feelings of loneliness (Hochschild, 1973; Gold, 1987; Connidis, 2001). Unmarried and/or childless older people, but particularly older women (Chambers 2005; 2006), are most likely to report feelings of satisfaction resulting from continuity of family practices and relationships with siblings.

By contrast, abrupt discontinuity in later life resulting from an irrevocable breakdown of relationships with a sibling is likely to have negative consequences for subsequent well-being, challenging as it does a previously accepted sibling identity derived from individual and familial biography and the presumed connectedness and family practices associated with that biography. Hilda's story is illustrative of this (female, aged 82, in Chambers, 2006). She recounted her upbringing in a large family of siblings and half-siblings: her mother had married twice but had worked hard to ensure that all her children regarded themselves as one family. Hilda was one of the younger members of the family and, while she was particularly close to two older half-sisters, she had continued to value the supportive and companionable relationships she had with all her brothers and sisters during early and late adulthood. In recent years, however, there had been a significant falling-out within the family when her two half-sisters had died without leaving wills. Her remaining half-brother had claimed the estate, stating that he was the only remaining 'true' family and furthermore he and his (now deceased) brother and sisters had always felt this way:

> It was so hurting, we had all been brought up together as brothers and sisters, no difference at all but when he came out with this remark and involved the other brother ... we were one family, that was how she brought us up, as one family ... it was the fact that he turned round and said 'You are not my brother and sister', that was what hurt me and it still does ... (in Chambers, 2006)

For Hilda, her identity as a sibling, located within a way of doing and being family, had thus been severely compromised and she was struggling to manage the uncertainties that resulted from that discontinuity. Her lack of connectedness continued to trouble her and affect her well-being, both in the present and potentially in the future. It is not surprising, therefore, that many older people, when talking about their siblings, stress the importance of resolving conflicts before it is too late to do so. As Win (female, aged 83) so eloquently demonstrates, the connectedness and continuity that comes from her sibling relationships enables her to face the future, and, indeed, her own mortality:

> You make friends throughout life but of course they start to die. And if your brothers and sisters are still alive, well they have been constant figures in your life. I was reading an essay by Robert Louis Stevenson and he said life is like a big frozen pond. The very thick ice is crowded with people and as you skate further on the ice gets thinner and some people fall through the ice. As it gets even thinner, you go through too. And you'll be skating alone on the last bit ... I'm on the thin ice but I'm not alone because the whole family ... are there with me on this ice. (in Chambers, 2006)

Conclusion

Of all the relationships that we discuss in this book, the sibling relationship is the one that, as a result of its longevity, is most embedded in individual and collective biography and family practices. It offers mutuality, and perhaps a greater possibility of equality, than many other family relationships in later life. Being or having a sibling potentially makes an important contribution to the maintenance of both identity and well-being at a time when identity may be perceived to be under threat. Reminiscence, in particular recounting of stories of shared events and remembered ways of doing family, validates and cements a connectedness with family of origin. Indeed, sibling relationships potentially provide links with and between the past, present and future. Significantly, it would seem also that for some older people their current relationship with siblings enables them to manage their own ageing process better and ultimately their own future mortality. By contrast, for others a lack of collective reminiscence, different perspectives on the past or, as in Hilda's family, broken bonds, affects well-being and perhaps makes the past, present and future even more uncertain.

SIX

Grandparenting

Introduction

Over the last 20 years grandparental relationships have received a good deal of attention from social scientists, especially in North America (eg Cherlin and Furstenberg, 1992; Szinovacz, 1998; Rosenthal and Gladstone, 2000; Attias-Donfut and Segalen, 2002; Crosnoe and Elder, 2002; Gauthier, 2002). One factor that generated interest in these ties was a growing awareness of the surprisingly high amount of full-time and part-time care that some grandmothers (and to a lesser extent grandfathers) were routinely involved in, especially in instances where parental care was problematic or lacking, for whatever reason (Minkler, 1999; Goodman and Silverstein, 2001). Overall, in the context of continuing claims about contemporary family decline, research tended to focus on the emotional and material contribution that grandparents made to their grandchildren's well-being, as well as on how grandparents acted as a family resource for the 'middle' generation of adult children/parents.

The findings reported in these recent studies resonate in some ways with the conclusions reached about grandparental involvement in mid-20th-century studies of traditional working-class localities. In these, intergenerational female kinship networks were often identified as central to domestic and familial organisation. Certainly many of the best-known British family and community studies of the period demonstrated the routine ways in which grandparents provided parents with help with young children, through childcare provision, the giving of gifts and/or providing advice about child-rearing practice (eg Young and Willmott, 1957; Rosser and Harris, 1965; Bell, 1968; Leonard, 1980). However, even if grandparental support for the second and third generation has an established history, certain features of contemporary grandparenting are significantly different from those characteristic of much of the 20th century. Two issues are particularly important.

First, the social, demographic and economic circumstances of grandparents have been altering. Not only do people typically first become grandparents at a relatively youthful age – currently by their early 50s, though recent childbearing patterns are beginning to alter this – but equally many do not now live near to their children, many are in full-time employment and many have active work, social and leisure lives of their own. Consequently the 'space' they have in their lives for 'doing grandparenting' is likely to be more restricted than it was in the past, especially for women. Second, the demography of household formation and dissolution has altered radically over the last 30 years. Increased divorce rates, cohabitation, lone parenthood and remarriage have had major repercussions not just for family as households but also for family as kinship. Undoubtedly these trends have structured the opportunities and possibilities that grandparents have to engage with their grandchildren, and to this extent have modified understandings of what grandparenting involves.

As this suggests, there is a great deal of diversity in the circumstances of grandparents and, consequently, in the relationships they construct with their grandchildren. While analysing commonalities in the character of grandparental relationships is important, it is also crucial to understand differences across these relationships and to identify the influences that shape the variations in them. Key here are not only the range of social and material factors that pattern the everyday lives of the different generations, but also such factors as the history of their relationships, the comparative ages of the grandparents and grandchildren, the effects of the family networks they are involved in, including other grandchildren and grandparents, and the other interests and responsibilities they all have (Mueller and Elder, 2003). This list could be extended, if not quite ad infinitum, then certainly at considerable length. The key issue is that, like other family relationships, these ties do not follow a set normative pattern. They may be framed by cultural understandings of how such relationships are appropriately constructed, but nonetheless the way grandparenting is done in practice is negotiated, in Finch and Mason's (1993) sense, between the individuals in the family network, with agency and structure both influential in the outcomes.

There is one key factor that has not yet been discussed. This is gender. While we can talk of grandparenting in a general sense, especially where the emphasis is on generational and lifecourse issues, the reality is that grandmothering and grandfathering are typically patterned in distinct ways (Clarke and Roberts, 2004). In other words, the relationships that grandchildren have with their grandmothers and grandfathers frequently take different trajectories, especially when the grandchildren are young. In large part this is a consequence of the structuring of gender identities, particularly in the context of family life. Overall, the greater responsibilities that women typically have for domestic organisation and family relationships result in grandmothers being more concerned with, and actively involved in, the unexceptional routines of grandchildren's early lives. It is also worth noting here that the gender of the intermediate parent is often of consequence too. As in the studies of traditional working-class localities referred to above, through providing practical and emotional support for their daughters, maternal grandmothers frequently participate more actively in their grandchildren's lives than paternal grandmothers do. (It is also possible that grandparents have different relationships with granddaughters and grandsons, though little research has focused specifically on this.)

The rest of this chapter is organised into four main sections. In the first of these, we will focus on the demography of grandparenthood. We will then examine the nature of grandparental commitment and solidarity, including the variations there are in this. Third, we will address changing patterns of grandparental involvement over the lifecourse. And finally we will consider the role of step-grandparents in their step-grandchildren's lives.

The demography of grandparenthood in the UK

As we have already noted, popular images of elderly grandparents are only partially accurate. In Clarke and Roberts' (2004) study of nearly 900 grandparents, the youngest was 37 and the oldest 94. As they point out: 'These grandparents were not the stereotypical old and retired family member; one third were under 60 and another third between 60 and 69 years old, and many were in paid employment' (Clarke and Roberts, 2004: 195). Clearly 37 is an unusually young age to become a grandparent. But, given that the average age of first births for women born in the early 1950s was 24 and the average of first birth for those born in the mid-1970s was 26 (ONS, 2004), many women born in the early 1950s could expect to be a grandparent in their late 40s or very early 50s. Similarly, many men born at that time first became a grandparent by their mid-50s. In line with this, on the basis of their nationally representative sample, Dench and Ogg (2002) report that the age at which over half of the population are grandparents is currently 54. Over the last 30 years birth patterns have been altering. Women are having children at a later age – in 2006 average age at first birth was close to 28 – and greater numbers are choosing not to have children at all. As a result, the average age at which people become grandparents for the first time will be increasing.

The vast majority of people who become grandparents remain so until their death, a period that, as Dench and Ogg (2002) point out, is likely to be over 20 years for grandfathers and 30 years for grandmothers. Dench and Ogg also provide data on the proportions of people of different ages who are grandparents and the number of grandchildren they have. From their analysis, the average number of grandchildren that the typical grandparent has is between four and five. For grandparents over the age of 60 the average is slightly over five, but from then on the number changes relatively little, reflecting the age at which their children typically complete their own childbearing phase of life. Only 1 in 20 grandparents now have 10 or more grandchildren, a much lower proportion than two generations ago.

As grandparents age, so of course do their grandchildren. Grandchildren's ages range from birth to occasionally over 60 (Silverstein and Marenco, 2001), with many individuals now having at least one grandparent alive when they are in their 30s. Recognising this immediately brings into focus the importance of a lifecourse perspective. The relationships that grandparents have with their grandchildren will be influenced by the changing circumstances of the grandparents' own lives, and also by the lifecourse position of their different grandchildren. While the forms of relationship that are developed when grandchildren are young – including the sense of commitment, solidarity and love established – are likely to influence those sustained as the grandchildren become adult, the patterns of interaction and the actual exchanges such interaction entails will clearly alter as the grandchildren become increasingly independent, both socially and economically.

As noted in the introduction to this chapter, other demographic changes of the last 30 years have also had an impact on grandparenting. In particular the growth of divorce and re-partnering, both among the grandparental and the parental generations, has had consequences for grandparental ties, as has the increased incidence of unmarried/unpartnered births. We will explore the significance of these changes for grandparental ties below, though research into these matters is quite limited. Clearly, though, the changes there have been in births, marriages and partnerships in recent years are altering the experiences of large numbers of grandparents and grandchildren. In Clarke and Roberts' (2004) study, nearly two out of five of the grandparents in their sample had at least one set of grandchildren whose parents were no longer living together, while for 10% of their respondents this was so for all their sets of grandchildren.

The doing of grandparenting/the ties that bind

'Grandchildren? Well, yes, there of course is the real tie.' This quote is by Griffith Hughes, a respondent in Rosser and Harris's classic kinship study *The family and social change* (1965: 8) undertaken in Swansea in the early 1960s. In many regards such sentiments remain central to an understanding of the character of grandparental relationships (Charles et al, 2008). There is a general acceptance of commitment and solidarity, with grandparents recognised as having a legitimate interest in their grandchildren. This interest encompasses both the positive feelings that grandparents are seen as 'naturally' having for their grandchildren, and in turn a belief that grandparents have a legitimate right to be involved with their grandchildren. That is, cultural understandings of the intergenerational 'blood' connection involve expectations of grandparental knowledge, involvement and concern, even though these can be expressed in quite different forms. Thus family practices may differ and relationships may be negotiated in diverse ways, but the underlying and largely taken-for-granted premise is that grandparents and grandchildren will have an enduring and active connection.

As noted, many factors affect the actual relationship that grandmothers and grandfathers have with their different grandchildren. One of consequence is that, like other kin ties, grandparental relationships are influenced by the character of the relationships sustained by intermediary kin. Thus the relationships between grandparents and parents are normally crucial in shaping grandparent–grandchildren ties (Mueller and Elder, 2003). When grandparents and parents are more involved in each other's lives, it is likely that grandparents and grandchildren will also have active relationships with each other. Conversely, where there is a less involved relationship between first and second generation, the tie between the first and third is also likely to be less close. As discussed below, this becomes particularly relevant when parents separate or divorce or otherwise do not live together. In these instances grandparent–grandchild relationships are likely to be affected by the character of the ties between the residential parent, on the one hand, and the non-residential parent and/or his/her parents, on the other.

The taken-for-granted solidarity expected of grandparents is expressed in a wide variety of ways. As Dench and Ogg (2002) report, some grandparents, and grandmothers especially, took quite a traditional role, with family being highly pertinent in their lives. They were in regular contact with their children, had positive relationships with their grandchildren, knew a great deal about their lives, and in many mundane ways expressed close as well as enduring solidarity. Other relationships between grandparents and grandchildren were less involved at an everyday level, while still being regarded as positive and supportive. In these families, there is an acceptance that appropriate solidarity can be expressed without such high degrees of contact, information flow or practical service. A small minority of grandparents have very limited involvement with their grandchildren, sometimes as a result of conflict between the first and second generations, and at other times because the grandparents choose lifestyles in which intergenerational involvement is a low priority (Cherlin and Furstenberg, 1992).

Clarke et al (2005) examine the types of family support that grandparents provide, distinguishing between practical, financial and emotional support. The nature and extent of the different support given depends on the circumstances of the different generations, as well as on the relationships that emerge over time. The idea of 'being there' for their children and grandchildren seems quite central to many grandparents' understanding of their role, though exactly what being there entails is generally ill-defined (Ferguson et al, 2004). Clearly, the ability to provide practical help, especially with regard to childcare, is constrained by geographical distance, among other things, as well as the different needs of the families involved. Material support, on the other hand, does not require geographical proximity in the same way, though the flow of resources varies widely, depending on the financial positions of the generations. As Clarke et al (2005) discuss, many grandparents choose to buy their grandchildren 'extras' and luxuries, whether small or large. Others contribute more to necessities for their grandchildren. Either way, as Bell (1968) long ago argued, such gifts and presents act as a means of expressing solidarity and ensuring continued involvement without undermining the independence of the adult generations.

This is an important issue in the construction of grandparental relationships, for while wanting to play a part in their grandchildren's lives, grandparents are also generally mindful of the normative significance of generational independence. In other words, as Mason et al (2007) have argued, grandparents often experience a degree of ambivalence between their desire to be there for their grandchildren and the recognition that they should not be seen as interfering. This can at times be a delicate balance, with the different family members involved having diverse ideas about when appropriate levels of support overstep the mark into interference (see also Chapter Seven). In turn, of course, some grandparents may at times feel that too much is being demanded of them. While they love their grandchildren, they do not always want to be on call or to act as substitute parents. The key issue here is that the balance between being there for their grandchildren and interfering is complex. How it is negotiated will vary between families as well as over time, reflecting both relational histories and existing family practices.

In principle, all grandparents are seen as having a natural interest in their grandchildren. However, the rise in divorce rates over the last two generations has had a significant effect on this otherwise presumed reality, as to a lesser extent has the rise of non-married motherhood and the incidence of cohabitation. When children are adult or in later adolescence at the time of their parents' separation, their relationships with their grandparents may not be much altered. When children are still young, though, the relationship they have with their (non-residential) grandparents is likely to be influenced by the character of the relationship they sustain with their non-residential parent. If they have a continuing relationship with their non-residential parent, they are also likely to maintain an active relationship with this parent's parents (Ferguson et al, 2004). Where the son or daughter has re-partnered, such grandparent–grandchild interaction is usually dependent upon the routine organisation of family life in the same ways as other grandparent–grandchild relationships normally are. However, because the parent in question happens not to be as fully involved with his or her children at a day-to-day level as residential parents are, this has obvious consequences for the timing and coordination of their meetings. Similar patterns are evident among non-residential fathers who have not re-partnered, though they are more likely to use their parents, and especially their mothers, as a childcare resource (see Burgoyne and Clark, 1984).

In some cases, relationships between grandchildren and their grandparents on their non-residential parent's side are affected more radically by separation and divorce. In particular, if a non-residential parent – typically the father – loses contact with their children, this can also result in a severance of the relationship between the grandchildren and their grandparents on that parent's side. However, this does appear to have been a more common consequence of divorce and stepfamily formation a generation ago than it is now (Burgoyne and Clark, 1984; Bradshaw et al, 1999). Given the greater emphasis there has been in recent years on the role of fathers in children's lives following divorce (Smart et al, 2001), it is not surprising that fewer non-residential grandparents lose contact with their grandchildren following divorce. As Ferguson et al (2004) point out, though, the relationships that these non-residential grandparents have with their grandchildren are still likely to become more attenuated following divorce than is the case for residential – typically maternal – grandparental relationships. Indeed, frequently maternal grandparents become more involved in providing practical, financial and emotional support for their daughter and grandchildren in the period following separation and divorce.

In a minority of cases, relationships between non-residential grandparents and grandchildren is mediated not only by the ties the non-residential parent maintains with his or her parents and children, but also by the positive relationship that the residential parent maintains independently with his or, more usually, her ex-parents-in-law. The independent strength of these relationships normally stems from the solidarity generated between the mother and her parents-in-law when the marriage was still intact (Finch and Mason, 1990; Ferguson et al, 2004). However, a positive relationship during the marriage is not sufficient in itself to ensure this. Frequently the conflicts and tensions of marital separation also lead to a schism between in-laws, partly because of the tendency for the (grand)parents to be, in Ferguson et al's (2004: 89) terms, 'partisan' towards their own child in allocating blame for the separation. In a small number of cases, though, characterised by a mutual goodwill, these difficulties are surmounted. This longer-term commitment between the residential parent and her/his ex-parents-in-law facilitates the continuation of an active relationship between these grandparents and their grandchildren (Allan et al, 2008).

Grandparenting across the lifecourse

When people think of grandparenting, the image that comes to mind is probably one of older but still active adults spending time with young children. This is the typical image presented in advertisements and other media and also the most common reality of more public settings of grandparenting. Yet, as we saw earlier, grandparental phases of the lifecourse are much broader than this implies. Some people become grandparents comparatively early in their lives; other relatively late. Even if we take the 'average' grandparent, their experience of grandparenting is likely to extend over a 20- to 30-year period. In other words, the relationships that they have with their grandchildren are not static; as each side ages so the nature of their interactions will also alter. Moreover, the emergent understandings that grandparents and grandchildren have of their relationship with each other are likely to differ, with each side viewing it from their own structurally distinct perspective (Dench and Ogg, 2002).

For most grandparental relationships, the grandchildren's early years are likely to be particularly important. It is at this time that ways of doing grandparenting are constructed, with these early modes influencing the ways that the relationships develop as each side ages. In general, from the child's perspective, the grandparent simply becomes part of their familial landscape, seen more or less routinely and being more or less involved in their different activities. Whatever their interactional patterns actually are, effectively their grandparents are part of the world that the child comes to take as given. Different grandparents will construct different involvements with the grandchild; in turn the grandchild will come to understand their different grandparents as distinct figures with their own personalities and ways of being.

The different modes of grandparenting that emerge are influenced by a range of contextual factors. They clearly depend on matters such as the frequency of contact, geographical distance and the grandparents' work, domestic and other commitments. But equally, the relationships that develop are rooted in – but in turn partially constitutive of – the sets of family practices that are characteristic of these families more generally. That is, the patterning of grandparental relationships with young children will reflect the histories of the relationships between the parents and the grandparents, the styles of doing family that have emerged, the commitments and antagonisms that exist, the 'moral reputations' (Finch and Mason, 1993) of those involved, and so on (see also Chapter Three). In turn, the ways in which the different grandparents express their interest in their grandchildren and the forms of support they provide for the parents (and especially the mother as typical main carer) will feed into future understandings of what can be expected of the different grandparents as they do their grandparenting. In this way, they become components within the dynamic yet routine construction of grandparental relationships within any particular family.

Importantly, it is in these ways that differences between grandmothers and grandfathers emerge. The gendered character of childcare, domestic labour and other family practices result in grandmothers typically being more proficient, knowledgeable and trusted than grandfathers as regards the care of young children. As a consequence they are more readily drawn into the 'mothering' of very young grandchildren than grandfathers are. From very early on, their experience and support is seen as particularly pertinent. Even when a grandmother and grandfather visit their grandchildren together, it is usually the grandmother who becomes more actively involved in the routine care of the children, with grandfathers taking more of a backseat, a process that continues in its different ways as the children become older. In addition, of course, many grandmothers actually see their grandchildren more frequently than grandfathers do, in part because of differential employment responsibilities. For similar reasons related to the gendered character of family life, maternal grandparents are usually more involved in grandchildren's lives than paternal ones. This is by no means inevitable, but the tendency of new mothers to turn to their own mothers for support has consequences for the emergent relationship between the grandparents and the grandchildren (Dench and Ogg, 2002; Ferguson et al, 2004).

As grandchildren get older, their relationship with their grandparents modifies. The solidarity that exists between them, consequent upon the ways the relationships were structured when they were younger, generally continues, but the content of their interactions is liable to be less extensive. Indeed, as the children become more independent different forms of involvement will emerge, with more active engagement, such as play and entertainment, giving way to more passive forms, perhaps especially talk about relatively mundane events in the child's life. At the same time, there is often an increased flow of gifts and other material resources, usually small but sometimes larger, directly to the child. As with other material exchanges, these serve to mark off the grandparental–grandchild bond as special and express the continuing love and solidarity between the generations.

Of course, these relationships do not alter only as a consequence of the grandchildren's changing social location. As the grandchildren age, so do the grandparents, with consequences for their personal and social circumstances. Allowing for the wide variation there is in the age difference between grandparents and grandchildren, many grandparents will be approaching the final phases of their life as their grandchildren reach adulthood. The majority of grandchildren in their mid-20s are likely to have grandparents who are 75 or older, and given contemporary childbearing patterns this age span will increase. Some grandparents may be widowed already and others becoming increasingly infirm.

As these processes occur, the nature of the exchanges between grandparents and grandchildren will shift further (Dench and Ogg, 2002; Kemp, 2005). For example, grandchildren may now visit grandparents more in the grandparents' homes, though more frequently intergenerational solidarity is expressed through the conduit of the intermediate parental generation. One example would be of grandchildren being at the parents' home when a grandparent visits. Another is through the parents providing a flow of information upwards and downwards. In other words, while there may at times be comparatively little direct interaction between the grandparent and the grandchild, the commitment and solidarity that exists is expressed through the interest each takes in the other's welfare. Similarly at this phase of the lifecourse, family rituals and ceremonies − birthdays, religious festivals, weddings and the like − provide occasions in which intergenerational family connection is reinforced.

Step-grandparents

As noted, contemporary patterns of separation, divorce and re-partnering have contributed to the emergence of more complex kinship configurations. Part of this is the presence in some family networks of step-grandparents whose involvement with the third generation is normally premised on different forms of commitment and solidarity than that of 'blood' grandparents. As Rosenthal and Gladstone (2000) note, step-grandparenthood is becoming an increasingly common experience within families, but one about which there has been rather little research. In this section we draw on a recent study concerned with step-grandparenthood undertaken by Allan and his colleagues (see Allan et al, 2008; forthcoming). Examining step-grandparenthood is not only interesting in its own right but also in what it reveals about the nature of blood grandparenthood.

As with blood grandparenthood, there is a good deal of variation in the way step-grandparental ties develop, though there are also some commonalities. To begin with, it is worth distinguishing two forms of step-grandparenthood. The first of these is where the re-partnership involves the intermediary parental generation; and the second is where the re-partnering involves one or more of the blood grandparents. In some of these latter cases, involvement between the step-grandparent and step-grandchild can be quite limited. This is obviously so when there is no relationship between the child's parent and the grandparent following the latter's divorce. It may also be the case when the new (grandparental) partnership has been formed relatively recently. These relationships tend to be more fully 'grandparental' when the remarriage or re-partnering has a more established history. In particular, when the step-grandparent acted as a step-parent during the parent's own childhood, the step-grandparent often forms part of a grandparental 'package' with the blood grandparent and is assigned the status of honorary natural grandparent. Indeed, in some instances like this in Allan et al's (2008) study, the grandchildren involved seemed relatively unaware that a step-relationship existed.

Step-grandparental relationships that develop as a result of a (now adult) child becoming a step-parent are generally comparatively unimportant in terms of kinship solidarity and commitment. Despite the variation there is in their patterning, these step-grandparents and step-grandchildren usually play only a small part in each other's lives. However, the particular relationships that develop are structured by the circumstances in which they emerge: for example, the length of time the step-family has existed, the age of the children when it was formed and the presence or otherwise of blood grandchildren in the same household as the step-grandchildren can all influence the ways step-grandparental ties develop. Yet, even allowing for the diversity that exists, step-grandparental relationships are normally seen as separate and distinct from the ties that bind blood grandparents and grandchildren.

In other words, while there is usually recognition of a mediated kin tie – these people are the parents of one's mother's or father's partner, or conversely the children of a child's partner – those involved are not usually defined as full members of the individual's own kin universe. There is little sense of commonality, connection or commitment, and limited involvement, except through the intermediary second generation (Coleman et al, 1997; Allan et al, 2008). In the main, unlike blood grandparents, they remain on the fringes of each other's lives. The step-grandparental tie is especially likely to be defined as incidental when the parental re-partnering occurs after a step-grandchild has become adult. The ensuing relationship with that partner's parents may be cordial, but it is unlikely to be seen as a family one. Indeed, in Allan et al's (2008) study, this was generally so if the grandchild was beyond their early teens when the new partnership was formed. In these cases a sense of family connection was rarely reported.

However, Allan et al (2008) found that a more kinship-relevant relationship sometimes develops between a step-grandparent and a step-grandchild if the child is still dependent at the time the new (parental) partnership is formed. For this to happen, though, it is usually also necessary for the stepchild and step-parent to live in the same household (Cherlin and Furstenberg, 1994). This is not really surprising as normally a non-residential step-parent's parents will have little opportunity or reason to become active in the stepchild's life. Indeed, generally they may not even meet that frequently. Principally this is because contact between the step-parent and his or her parents and between the step-parent and his or her non-residential stepchildren is usually organised so as not to overlap. In other words, if a child is spending time with a non-residential parent, that time is often set aside for servicing and sustaining that relationship, rather than involving 'outsiders' – which, in kinship terms, is generally how the step-grandparents are perceived. If other kin ties outside the household are to be involved during these contact times, precedence is routinely given to the blood grandparents (or aunts, uncles and cousins) on the non-residential parent's side rather than to the step-grandparents (or other step-relatives).

Overall it seems that relationships between step-grandparents and step-grandchildren only come to be understood as grandparental in any significant sense if a stepchild is young and living in the household with their step-parent at the time when the stepfamily is formed. Even here, though, there is usually a strong consciousness that these relationships are different from the ones sustained with blood grandchildren/grandparents. Indeed, in Allan et al's (2008) study, while some grandparents appeared to make a conscious effort to *treat* all their grandchildren similarly, often they indicated they *felt* differently about their blood grandchildren. In reality, these feelings themselves usually resulted in differential treatment, so that in practice the boundaries between blood grandparenthood and step-grandparenthood continued to be evident. Indeed, Allan et al (2008) reported that the only instances in their sample of the step-grandparent/step-grandchild tie being fully construed as grandparental arose when a step-parent had taken on parental responsibility for infants or very young children – where in effect they had 'replaced' the natural parent in the child's life from an early age.

These issues underscore the character of blood grandparental relationships. Being a blood grandparent involves a level of connection, interest and emotional attachment that cannot easily be forged with other children who are not part of one's blood. Rather than representing a shared heritage, step-grandparental relationships are usually seen as contingent, with continuing interaction dependent on circumstances rather than deliberate agency. That is, instead of being sustained for their own sake, they were relationships that were consequent on the relationship a parent or adult child happened to have with his or her partner. This difference highlights the taken-for-granted solidarity so characteristic of blood grandparental ties. Step-grandparents lack the commitment of blood grandparents and do not have the same level of interest or right to involvement in their lives.

Conclusion

In concluding this chapter, we want to highlight three issues. First, as we keep emphasising, there is much variation in the character of grandparental relationships, with many different factors influencing their patterning. However, in the main, behind these variations lies a common acceptance that there will be solidarity and commitment between grandparents and their grandchildren, a solidarity and commitment that is often portrayed as natural. As we have argued here, that commitment is expressed in different ways depending on both the circumstances of those involved and the history of family relationships in which they are mutually embedded. Moreover these relationships are not static or given; they inevitably alter over time. Thus not only are they emergent and negotiated ties but they are also ties in which both ageing and lifecourse position play a key part.

Second, one of the key influences patterning grandparental relationships is the network of kinship ties in which they are embedded (Mueller and Elder, 2003). Thus the relationships between grandparents and grandchildren, especially but not only while the grandchildren are dependent, are mediated through the intermediate relationships involved. Grandchildren can help cement these relationships and give them additional 'content', but these ties — between parents and their children and their children's spouses/partners — have their own histories and dynamics that inevitably impinge on the ways that grandparent–grandchildren ties are constructed. Similarly, grandparental relationships are affected by the partnership status of the parental relationship. As we have seen, separation and divorce tend to alter the opportunities there are for grandparental involvement, particularly for the grandparents whose child no longer lives with the grandchild(ren). Equally, recent increases in cohabitation and births to unpartnered mothers also render some grandparental ties more complex to negotiate.

Finally, we want to emphasise the 'normality' of grandparental involvement in family life. As discussed in the Introduction, older people are often portrayed as socially and physically dependent, the recipients of support and concern. For some in later old age their needs for care are of course comparatively high. However, for most, most of the time, this is a misrepresentation of the exchanges family life entails. As we have tried to show, grandparents are not only a significant resource in their children's and grandchildren's lives, they are also an integral element within the complex of family practices that different families establish. The so-called 'extended family' of common lament is frequently misconstrued as being essentially a three-generation household. Such households are comparatively rare. What is not rare is for grandparents and grandchildren to be highly significant in each other's kinship landscapes. In this fuller sense, extended families certainly live on.

SEVEN

Later life widow(er)hood

Introduction

This chapter argues for a lifecourse approach to understanding family practices in later life in relation to later life widow(er)hood. A lifecourse perspective takes the view that continuing and accumulative experiences over the lifecourse influence the experience of family relationships and practices in later life (Hockey and James, 2003). Gender is fundamental to this discussion of the way in which older widows and widowers 'do' family (Davidson, 2001); indeed, as argued by Morgan (1996: 11), family practices and gendered practices are likely to overlap. This chapter will argue that cohort, linked to gender, is an equally important component in understanding the way in which the loss of a partner affects family practices that have been developed over the lifecourse (Chambers, 2005). This chapter will consider how for many older women, in particular, notions of 'home' become reinforced as a site for family practices in widow(er)hood and how for some older widows and widowers life after the death of their spouse results in a juxtaposition of both old and new ways of 'being' and 'doing'. The potential impact on family practices of different ways of re-partnering will be explored, including living apart together (LAT) relationships.

A lifecourse approach to later life widow(er)hood

The transition to widow(er)hood is an expectation of later life, particularly for older women. As De Jong Gierveld (2003) reminds us, this does not necessarily lessen its impact on the remaining spouse: partner and family relationships are major integrating structures in society and individuals without a partner are more likely to be lonely than those with a partner. Indeed, a powerful mythology suggests that loneliness is the *automatic* consequence of later life widow(er)hood. Some years ago Adlersberg and Thorne (1992: 9) commented: 'The vast quantity of literature on older widows in our society convincingly portrays widowhood as an experience fraught with poverty, ill-health, loneliness, grief and re-adjustment.'

Such taken-for-granted knowledge still perpetuates this mythology, with widow(er)hood being blamed for many of the ills of later life (Chambers, 2009). However, a lifecourse perspective on later life widow(er)hood argues that the way in which the 'event' of losing a spouse is both experienced and subsequently managed is rooted in the personal, social and collective biography of an individual and her/his family (Martin-Matthews, 1991; 1999; Chambers, 2005). While recognising the potential disruption of the death of a spouse, we should be careful not to focus on the discontinuity of the event at the expense of major continuities embedded in an individual's lifecourse. Not unexpectedly, given the complex nature of such continuities, later life widow(er)hood is extremely variable and is made up of a wide spectrum of experience. For some older women in particular it is a time of potential opportunity, or what has been described by a number of commentators as 'a transition' (Davidson, 1999; Martin-Matthews, 1999; Chambers, 2005). These women may draw on skills, opportunities and resources located within their personal and collective biography, previous relationships with others and a realisation that their life does not have to stand still. For them, widowhood offers new ways of 'being'. However, for those at the other end of the spectrum it may be experienced as a time of extreme vulnerability and misery. For these women, the continuities that they bring to later life widowhood are unhelpful and even disabling in the face of the discontinuities of widowhood itself (Matthews, 1979). For example, lifelong low self-esteem and a lack of social identity, feeling different from others, dependence on family and so on may all play their part in reinforcing feelings of hopelessness that may in their turn be perpetuated by current family relationships. For those who have experienced an unhappy or abusive marriage, widowhood may be a blessed relief, a time of release from a domineering spouse: 'Life changed. It is much quieter now. Since my husband was an alcoholic, life was not easy before he died' (older widow, in Martin-Matthews, 1991: 18–19).

Of course, not all family members may share this view and in a climate in which life after the death of a spouse suggests otherwise, it may be extremely difficult for some older people to express satisfaction. Indeed, some of the older women interviewed by Adlersberg and Thorne (1992) and Chambers (2005) had felt unable – for fear of censure – to share their feelings of relief with close family; they welcomed with enthusiasm the opportunity to talk freely about the positive aspects of widowhood. Perhaps not surprisingly, having internalised taken-for-granted knowledge about expectations of widowhood, the women also reported feelings of guilt at sharing such satisfaction and relief.

Gender

The experience of widow(er)hood is of course not gender neutral: gendered relationships in widow(er)hood reflect the gendered nature of society (Connidis, 2001; Davidson, 2001; Chambers, 2005; Hall et al, 2007). There is a general consensus that although older women are more likely to experience financial disadvantage (Arber and Ginn, 1991), largely as a result of financial deficits accrued over the lifecourse, and chronic ill-health (Gibson, 1996), they are more likely to fare better in widow(er)hood than older men because of their lifelong capacity to garner and maintain social relationships and kinship ties (Connidis, 2001). As widows, they thus have access to a vast range of relationships embedded in lifelong social networks (adult children and grandchildren, siblings and siblings-in-law, cousins, old friends and so on). In addition, new opportunities for friendship and companionship present themselves as a result of gaining entry into what Lopata (1973; 1996) described as 'a society of widows': a world in which, because of greater longevity and a propensity to marry men older than themselves, older women predominate. Indeed, new types of friendships with widowed sisters and sisters-in-law are often reported.

By contrast, older widowers are much more likely to have a smaller social network to draw upon. Davidson et al (2003: 177) suggest that this is because men are much more likely than women to lodge all their emotional investment with their partner. Furthermore, there is no equivalent 'society of widowers' for older men to tap into. Most researchers would agree that, by comparison with older widows, older widowed men are more limited in terms of developing and maintaining relationships with family and friends, less experienced in domestic tasks and have a high potential for loneliness (see for example, Connidis, 2001).

Perhaps not surprisingly, older women and men confirm this gendered view of 'who fares best', drawing on what Cancian (cited in Davidson et al, 2003: 171) refers to as the 'feminine ruler'. For example, an older Australian widower (in Hall et al, 2007: 13) remarked: 'It strikes me that women handle [widowhood] better than men do for some reason, god knows why ... I think men will withdraw. They're not so likely to go out and find themselves a group.' Betty, an older widow (in Chambers, 2005: 221), reinforces this view: 'A lot of men ... need someone to lean on; they can't manage on their own. Some of them can but many can't. You see, I can manage.'

A study of North American older widowers (Moore and Stratton, 2001), in which older men spoke about their experience, found that most older widowers did indeed have 'someone to lean on' in later life widowerhood: nearly all the men at the time of interview had a significant, caring and sustaining relationship with a woman. Interestingly, the 'current woman' (Moore and Stratton, 2004: 21) was not necessarily a new wife but might be one of the following: adult daughter, neighbour, church member, sister/sister-in-law or daughter-in-law. These relationships enabled the men to manage widowerhood better by providing domestic support, companionship and, for some, the opportunity to maintain family activities, roles and responsibilities previously undertaken with their deceased spouse.

Drawing on a lifecourse perspective, we would, however, urge some caution in relation to gendered practices and social networks. Some older women, like many of their male counterparts, have indeed put all their emotional eggs in one basket and thus in widowhood find that they too have few social networks to draw upon. For those women who have also expressed loneliness and isolation in marriage, the death of a spouse may serve to further reinforce their lack of skills and confidence associated with developing relationships, even within their own family. Patricia (female, aged 67), for example, reflected ruefully:

> Once he started working nights, if you were ever asked to go anywhere
> ... you couldn't ... well they never asked you again. I don't know where

> half the people I used to know are and as I say when my husband
> started work nights, that put an end to it all, it does kill family life,
> I mean when other people are sat down all together of an evening,
> you are on your own ... When you get married, you lose friends, you
> lose contact with other people ... which is wrong I suppose. I made a
> lot of mistakes ... I was the lonely one and I am now. (in Chambers,
> 2005: 173)

For others, a sense of 'being different' from or holding negative attitudes to other
older women means that entry into a society of older women is not welcomed,
even when that world includes members of their own family. Vera (female, aged
67), for example, had spent a large part of her life in the predominantly male
world of the RAF, and had few female friends during that time:

> I always got on a lot better with men than with women ... in the
> officers' mess it was mainly men. I was always in a man's environment,
> I was always talking to men and very few women ... I think I'm a bit
> on my guard with women. My sister and I never really got on, and we
> still don't, I'm a bit wary. I've only ever had three close friends, one in
> New Zealand, one who died last year and my other school friend. It
> makes it difficult to extend friendships, I feel much easier with men.
> I don't think I'll change now. (in Chambers, 2005: 197–8)

Cohort

Cohort is an important feature of a lifecourse approach to the family in later
life, affecting both family and gender practices (Riley, 1973; Ruth and Oberg,
1995; Giele and Elder, 1998). This would apply to any cohort but, given the
confines of this chapter and this section, we focus on a specific cohort of men and
women. Chambers (2005), for example, used biographical interviews to explore
the experience of later life widowhood for a sample of women who identified
themselves as belonging to a cohort of the 'Second World War generation'. She
argued that the subjective experience of later life widowhood could only be really
understood via older women's narratives derived from collective (both as women
and of a specific cohort) and individual biographies rather than from the event of
widowhood itself. What these older widows' narratives tell us of family life over
the lifecourse, their priorities, their ways of doing family life and their capacity to
connect with other family members, as well as the way in which they construe
themselves to have been different from or the same as other families, enables us
to understand better their current family relationships and practices.

For all the women in Chambers' (2005) study, a dominant ideology of the family,
which encompassed both the institution of the family as 'good' and also women's
roles within the institution, was evident. Being 'the good wife and mother', as one
whose primary role and responsibility was to husband and family, was extremely

powerful in shaping their view of the world and their role within it. This was, of course, reinforced by social policy (Summerfield, 1989; Roberts, 1998).

> Well, there was no question of going to work, no question at all. Oh my goodness there was a home to be run and children and everything like that. Sometimes, if I grumbled about money he would say 'Well you can always get yourself a job ...', but he didn't mean it, oh no. My place was in the home. And there were many women like me. (Joan, female, aged 74, in Chambers, 2005: 157)

However, the way in which that ideology of the family was played out within families and its impact on current family practices was and continues to be extremely variable. Chambers (2005) found that ways of doing family could range from interdependence, family as friends, dependence through to a lack of closeness. Significantly, these lifelong ways of doing family underpinned the challenges and transitions faced by older widows, resulting in a juxtaposition of both continuity and discontinuity.

'Interdependence' described those families who maintained regular contact and interaction and 'looked out for each' other but led separate lives and maintained private space. Relationships were warm and friendly, and family occasions were celebrated, but in the normal course of social life they went their own way. Respect both of generational differences and autonomy of households was integral to this way of doing family. Jean (female, aged 72) put this succinctly:

> You can be too far away, but you can be too near, on both sides. As long as I'm within a distance that I can get there if they want me or they can get to me ... it's important to have friends of your own age as well as family. Different generations don't mix ... their outlooks are different. (in Chambers, 2005: 180)

By implication Jean, and others, were stressing a distinction between their family practices and those of friends.

Some older widows described their relationships with family as 'friendship' or 'companionship'. Often this involved long-standing mutual interests, often with daughters but sometimes also with sons, or sons-in-law. Relationships were warm and friendly, contact was frequent and regular but in contrast to interdependence, those who practised family as friends were happy to spend time together outside family occasions:

> [Having the boat together] was lovely. Although we were all really sick at heart because of [losing] Dad, we loved going to the boat ... my son-in-law would get off work early and we'd get off to the boat, get it all laid out, then we'd go up to Lymm and do the weekend shopping and

we'd go back to the boat with this shopping. It just filled all our time; it was marvellous (Joan, female, aged 74, in Chambers, 2005: 183)

Furthermore, those who did not practise family as friends were considered by this group of older widows to be at a disadvantage, particularly as they became more frail and perhaps less able to access other social activities. By contrast, a relationship of 'dependence' was not to be wished for. It was a relationship in which there had been, and continued to be a lack of reciprocity, an unequal balance of power and few shared interests. There may be frequent contact but notions of 'duty' dominated family practices: 'She takes on a lot of responsibility for me. She worries about me and I worry about her. That's the trouble, there's only the two of us ... my sister has her family to see to, I think she only comes here out of duty' (Patricia, female, aged 67, talking about her relationship with her daughter, in Chambers, 2005: 184). Such dependent family relationships potentially reduced agency and thus the capacity and energy to develop other relationships, often resulting, as these widows grew older, in extreme loneliness and isolation.

While still subscribing to the centrality of the family, and their role within it, there was nonetheless acknowledgement by some women that 'a lack of closeness' best described their current family relationships and influenced the way in which they interacted with each other. Family ties were no longer strong, contact had become increasingly more infrequent and there was a sense in which lifelong family practices had become less important than other aspects of their lives: whether this was always of their own choosing is debatable. Betty (female, aged 73), for example, talked about the way in which she felt increasingly distanced from her family: 'They've all got on with their own lives ... possibly we're not close, we're not a close family. When the children were little I used to see a lot more of them then ... but you see they've got other things to do and I do other things' (in Chambers 2005: 186).

Within Chambers' (2005) study there were a number of older widows who were childless. For these women, lifelong family practices had been extremely helpful in enabling them to manage a number of transitions and challenges as they faced a future without both husband and children. Edith for example (female, aged 64) belonged to a large but close family of sisters, brothers-in-law, nieces and nephews. During her married life she and her husband enjoyed spending time with her family, but 'made special time for' a younger, single (and also childless) sister when her other brothers and sisters were occupied with their own young families. They shared social activities and once a year went on holiday together. When she was first widowed, and experiencing considerable mental distress, Edith in turn received significant emotional and practical support from her younger sister. Since that time, although they maintain separate households, they have developed an even stronger relationship that has provided them both with companionship and new opportunities. They participate fully in wider family activities, and each has their own favourite nieces and nephews, but, importantly for them, they are not dependent on the family. They have become good friends who together are able to face the world outside. Indeed, at the time of the interview, they were planning a month's holiday to Canada. Lifelong family practices have provided continuity and have also enabled them both to combine old and new ways of being and doing.

Older widowers and still-married men of the same cohort who took part in research by Davidson et al (2003) also reflected the prevalent cohort and gendered expectations surrounding both paid work and childcare responsibilities, which meant these men had little time available to spend with their children, often resulting in a peripheral and less engaged role in family life. These older men acknowledged their wife's expertise in the domestic sphere and, by way of comparison, their own lack of skill in managing family life: keeping in touch with family, initiating family occasions, offering support, being able to show affection and so on. For example:

> I wasn't the sort of father who talked a lot. Some fathers talk a lot to their sons or daughters. I may have done more perhaps if it had been a girl. I don't know, it might have been different. No, I didn't talk to him a lot. He talked to his mother much more than me. (Gary, a widower, aged 80, in Davidson et al, 2003: 178)

This lack of expertise is often tacitly recognised by adult children, who are likely both to initiate contact and to offer instrumental support to their father when he is widowed. According to Davidson et al (2003), widowed persons are likely to spend more time with family members than those who are still married and for some widowers this offers the potential to develop stronger relationships with adult children – particularly with adult daughters – and to rekindle relationships with siblings (see Chapter Five). This is also true in relation to grandchildren. Many widowed men in the study reported that they now had a special relationship with their grandchildren. Davidson et al (2003: 179) speculate that the death of a grandmother provides opportunities for the grandfather to take on roles, such as babysitting, more commonly carried out by older women and, paradoxically offers the possibility of a closer relationship with grandchildren than might have been possible had their wife still been alive (see Chapter Six for further discussion of grandparenting). In the context of this chapter, we would argue that such possibilities – the development of new types of relationships with adult children, siblings and grandchildren – offer older widowers new ways of being and of doing family relationships.

Re-partnering

The final part of this chapter considers the effect of re-partnering on family practices. Davidson (2001) argues that re-partnering after widowhood is gender specific, with older widowers being more likely to seek out another partner for marriage (see also Van den Hoonaard, 2004). Statistically, of course, older men have a considerable advantage over older women. Indeed, Moore and Stratton (2004) have commented that all the men in their study could have remarried had they wished to. However, for older widowers loneliness rather than opportunity would appear to be the determining factor in choosing whether to remarry (Davidson, 2001; 2004; Moore and Stratton, 2004; Van den Hoonard, 2004). Older widows, by contrast, are more likely to choose to remain without a partner, largely from a desire to maintain their freedom (Davidson, 2001; 2004; Chambers, 2005). Jenny (female, aged 73), for example, reflected on turning down a proposal of marriage:

> I've had an offer, a professor from the university, we'd been married about the same length of time and been widowed. But I didn't want to ... marriage ties you down. I wouldn't want that again. Now if I want to ring a friend to do something I can. I've a lot of freedom now. Marriage restricts you, even if you have a happy marriage, and that's how it should be. If you marry someone it's because you want to be together. He's married now and I'm friends with his wife. Ada [friend] asks me if I feel I missed my chance ... but I don't feel I have, it's not what I want. (in Chambers, 2005: 221)

For many of those men who do remarry, their contact with their family is stronger. As Hagestad (1986) observed, over 20 years ago now, second wives kept men connected with their families in ways that men could not maintain on their own. This is echoed by Moore and Stratton (2004: 133), who refer to some of the second wives in their study as 'superlative kin-keepers': 'For example, Garrett's second wife had been a good friend of his first wife. He called out to her in a far room of the house several times when the interviewer asked about his children and their families.'

Re-partnering, by its very nature, creates new and diverse family structures and complex household patterns, and for some adult children the remarriage of an older parent may be a less than welcome event (Grinwald and Shabat, 1997; De Jong Gierveld and Peeters, 2003). They may see the new partnership as disrespectful to the memory of a deceased parent, may feel resentful about the use of the family home by a new partner as well as having anxieties about a previously anticipated inheritance (De Jong Gierveld and Peeters, 2003; Moore and Stratton, 2004). Remarriage may also bring with it challenges to long-lasting family practices. Not sharing a family biography, new partners may find it difficult to engage with existing ways of doing family:

> My children always respected and were always very good to him. When they were gone, he would always talk negatively about them. He found the grandchildren too noisy and told me time and time again that they didn't have good manners. My children never did anything right in his eyes. They did their best to put him at ease but

he found everything too much. (Female, aged 75, remarried, in De Jong Gierveld and Peeters, 2003: 191)

Increasingly, many older widows and some older widowers are choosing not to remarry. Instead, they are seeking flexible arrangements for re-partnering (Borell and Karlsson, 2003; De Jong Gierveld and Peeters, 2003; 2004). Older women in particular may seek to resist the 'burdens' (De Jong Gierveld, 2004: 87) involved in remarriage, especially in relation to domestic duties and responsibilities. Eunice (female, aged 69), for example, had given some consideration to a range of possibilities:

> I've missed male company. I mean some people actually approach dating agencies but I've never done that. I wouldn't want to marry again. I'd be quite happy 'living in sin' I think or just having a friendship with someone. I mean nowadays if I want to cook a full meal for myself I can but Laurie enjoyed his food and it would always have to be a proper meal for him and I don't think I'd want to do that again. (in Chambers, 2005: 221)

Pat (female, aged 66), while recognising that she too missed male company, was not prepared to take the risk of having a partner become too dependent on her:

> I would like a man to be friendly with. I've joined a 'singles club' ... It's just for people who are on their own to meet and have a friendly evening and it's for my age group more or less. It's nice to have a conversation with a man, different from women's conversations all the time. I wouldn't mind somebody to go with for a meal or something like that, but I'd never get married again. I couldn't be bothered with all the washing and I think if you get married young well you're used to each other's ways. Whereas when you are older, you're very set in your ways and it would be difficult to live with somebody again. And you also, even though you are on your own, you do get a certain independence that you really don't want to lose either. If you like, going somewhere ... you can go and you don't have to rush back. (in Chambers, 2005: 221–2)

De Jong Geerveld and Peeters (2003) and Borell and Karlsson (2003) have argued that it is primarily older women who are the driving force in the development of new forms of relationships in later life, particularly in the formation of LAT relationships. A LAT relationship is one in which both partners are loyal, committed and intimate but, although they may live together for short periods of time, and may share family activities, they maintain separate households, personal belongings and finances. This enables both partners to retain some of the continuities resulting from their respective, separate and individual biographies at the same time as embarking on a new, shared life together. This results in a juxtaposition of both old and new ways of being and doing. One of the interviewees in the NESTOR[1] survey recounted her reasons for embarking on a LAT relationship:

> After a period of living alone, you have fixed habits ... It is difficult to adjust ... if you are very old, you are a whole person, and it is difficult to change your habits [and] since we both have a life behind us ... it's much more difficult than starting from scratch ... He is an authoritarian type of person; he is always trying to determine what I should do. (Female, aged 71, 'living apart together', in De Jong Gierveld and Peeters, 2003: 190)

The maintenance of a separate family home seems particularly important for older widows, not just in terms of their independence but also in terms of their identity. In a small-scale indepth study that sought to understand how older women managed the uncertainties brought about by later widowhood, Porter (1995) argued for the centrality of 'home' in older widows' lives as a means of maintaining continuities and, for those women who had family, preserving both a history of and site for the maintenance of family practices.

For both older men and women in LAT relationships, provided the nature of the relationship is made clear, roles and relationships with older children are often less complicated and indeed more favourable, certainly in relation to 'inheritance':

> I want to stay independent ... an important consideration is that I only have one daughter (and a bit of money), and my partner has more children (and no money). A marriage would soon give rise to a lot of problems. I would rather give my money to my own children and great grandchildren. (Male, aged 85, 'living apart together', in De Jong Gierveld and Peeters, 2003: 192)

It would seem that for older widows and widowers, despite a commitment to change (in terms of a new relationship), when it comes to family norms and practices change does not happen at the expense of continuity; rather it takes place alongside it.

Conclusion

The family lives of older widows and widowers have the potential both to stay the same and to change; indeed, as we have shown in this chapter, change and continuity sit side by side in the lives of the older people whose experience we have discussed. Older widows and widowers engage in a variety of relationships, some old and some new, which are rooted in long-standing ways of doing family. What is certain is that those family practices are embedded in individual and collective biographies, in which both gender and cohort are fundamental.

Note

[1] NESTOR refers to 'Living arrangements and social networks of older adults', part of the Netherlands Programme for Research on Ageing, funded by the Ministry of Welfare, Health and Cultural Affairs.

EIGHT

Globalisation and transnational communities: implications for family life in old age

Introduction

This chapter considers some of the challenges raised by the development of globalisation for understanding changes to family life. Debates around the theme of globalisation became influential in the social sciences during the 1990s, notably in sociology and political science (Held et al, 1999). Subsequently, this work was to broaden out with extensive discussions both in social policy (George and Wilding, 2002) and social gerontology (Estes and Phillipson, 2002; Baars et al, 2006). Globalisation has now become an influential force in the construction of old age, notably so in the framing of social and economic policies designed to manage and regulate population ageing. Research on ageing can no longer be confined to local or national cultures, shaped as these are by a wider transnational context, with international organisations (such as the World Bank and International Monetary Fund) and cross-border migrations creating new conditions and environments that influence the lives of older people.

The main argument developed in this chapter is that the phenomenon of globalisation raises important new concerns for understanding family life in old age. In general, the focus on globalisation confirms the importance of locating individuals within the orbit of social and economic structures. Those are increasingly subject to forces lying beyond the boundaries of the nation state. This chapter will, first, summarise the main approaches to understanding globalisation within sociology and social policy; second, review the relevance of this approach for understanding family life; third, assess the importance of transnational families as a feature of global change; finally, it will review implications for social policy that come out of the rise of international migration.

Defining globalisation

Globalisation, it is argued in this chapter, will have a major influence on the future of family life – across all age groups. The term globalisation is taken to refer to those mechanisms, actors and institutions that link together individuals and groups across different nation states. David Held et al define globalisation in the following terms:

Today, virtually all nation-states have gradually become enmeshed in and
functionally part of a larger pattern of global transformations and global
flows ... Transnational networks and relations have developed across
virtually all areas of human activity. Goods, capital, people, knowledge,
communications and weapons, as well as crime, pollutants, fashions
and beliefs, rapidly move across territorial boundaries ... Far from this
being a world of 'discrete civilisations' or simply an international order
of states, it has become a fundamentally interconnected global order,
marked by intense patterns of exchange as well as by clear patterns of
power, hierarchy and unevenness. (Held et al, 1999: 49)

Globalisation brings forth a new set of actors and institutions that influence the
social construction of public policy for old age. To take one example, the increasing
power of global finance and private transnational bodies raises significant issues
about the nature of citizenship – and associated rights to health and social care
– in old age. In the period of welfare state reconstruction, rights were defined
and negotiated through various manifestations of nation state-based social policy.
Globalisation, however, transfers citizenship issues to a transnational stage; this
is driven by a combination of the power of intergovernmental structures, the
influence of multinational corporations and the pressures of population movement
and migration (Baars et al, 2006).

In general terms, globalisation has produced a distinctive stage in the history of
ageing, with tensions between nation state-based policies concerning demographic
change and those formulated by global actors and institutions. Social ageing
can no longer be viewed solely as a national problem or issue but as one that
affects individuals, groups and communities across the globe. Local and national
interpretations of ageing had substance where nation states (at least in the
developed world) claimed some control over the construction of welfare policies.
They also carried force where social policies were being designed with the aim or
aspiration of levelling inequalities, and where citizenship was still predominantly
a national issue. The changes affecting all of these areas, largely set in motion by
different aspects of globalisation, is likely to generate significant implications for
understanding changes in the family life of older people.

Globalisation and family life

For societies in the 21st century, communities of families and relations sustained
across wide geographical distances are likely to play an increasingly influential
role in daily life. The American demographer Douglas Massey (2000: 134) argues
that, barring some calamity or radical shift in family-planning trends, '[M]igration
will play a greater role than reproduction in determining the strength and tenor
of our societies.' Arising from the growth of international development are what
has been termed 'transnational communities' that play an increasingly influential
role in reshaping many aspects of family life. Transnational communities may be

said to arise from a context in which those who leave a country and those who stay remain connected through a variety of ties linked with different patterns of exchange and support (Basch et al, 1994).

One consequence of international migration is the rise of 'global' or 'transnational' families. Baldassar et al (2007:13) suggest that the idea of the transnational family 'is intended to capture the growing awareness that members of families retain their sense of collectivity and kinship in spite of being spread across multiple nations'. Arlie Hochschild (2000) argues that most writing about globalisation focuses on money, markets and flows of labour, with limited attention paid to women, children and the support that flows from one to the other. However, older people also experience international migration in a variety of ways: for example, as first-generation migrants growing old in their second homeland (Burholt, 2004); as a group left behind and coping with the loss of younger generations (Vullnetari and King, 2008); or as a group heavily involved in the practices associated with transnational care-giving (Baldassar et al, 2007).

International migration produces greater diversity in respect of the social networks within which growing old is shaped and managed. Typically, older people's networks have been examined within national borders with their need for care and support assessed within this context. But migrants bring important variations with responsibilities and resources that may stretch considerable physical distances. First-generation migrants may move between continents, maintaining economic and cultural as well as social ties across dispersed communities. The globalisation of family life is creating a major new research agenda in terms of tracking how generational ties are sustained across different nation states. Some of the key questions to be addressed here include: Are new means of contact and communication being developed to sustain traditional ties within families? What are the different ways in which men and women respond to the pressures of migration? Do distinctive types of reciprocity develop among families separated through time and place?

Globalisation and transnational communities

Peggy Levitt (2001: 4) suggests that the rise of the transnational community reflects 'how ordinary people are incorporated into the countries that receive them while remaining active in the places they come from'. Basch et al further define this relationship as follows:

> ... transnationalism [is] the process by which immigrants forge and sustain multi-stranded social relations that link together their societies of origin and settlement. We call these processes transnationalism to emphasize that many immigrants build social fields that cross geographic, cultural and political borders ... an essential element is the multiplicity of involvements that transmigrants sustain in home and host societies. (Basch et al, 1994: 6)

Portes and Bach (1985: 10) have described migration as a process of network building, which 'depends on and in turn reinforces social relations across time and space linking migrants and non-migrants'. This approach draws out the dynamic nature of the ties maintained through different stages of migration, variations between generations of migrants, and between male and female migrants. Women may in fact occupy a distinctive position within transnational communities. Khanum (1994) highlights their social and economic role in strengthening kinship ties, often to the detriment of their own social and economic needs. Drawing on her fieldwork in Bangladesh, she observes that:

> [The] kinship tie demands that women send money to the poor relatives of their husband in Bangladesh. Apart from these cases, women also have to contribute to relatives living in the UK even when they are supported by [income support] or from their own earnings, simply because of the prevailing norms. (Khanum, 1994: 296)

A major aspect of globalisation has been its impact on those who stay behind in the villages and cities of less-developed countries and those uprooted through international migration. Gulati's (1993) study, *In the absence of their men: The impact of male migration on women*, examined migration from the Indian state of Kerala to west Asia, noting the challenges facing women coping with managing alone with a new family, but with a long period of separation from a husband to whom they may have been married for just a few weeks. King and Vullnetari (2006) explored the effect of the mass migration of young people from Albania, most notably on those older people living in rural parts of the country. The study reports feelings of separation and abandonment among the older generation, heightened by the realisation that their children are unlikely to return (see, further, Vullnetari and King, 2008).

The Albanian case illustrates problems of maintaining ties with relatives who may have entered a destination country without any legal status, with their 'undocumented status making it difficult for them to return' to their homeland country (Vullnetari and King, 2008: 788). On the other hand, there are numerous examples in the literature of migrants moving backwards and forwards between their first and second homelands, subject to financial and domestic constraints. Goulborne (1999) in his study (see also Bauer and Thompson, 2006) highlights the back and forth movement of the Caribbean families living in Britain. Similar descriptions have been linked to first-generation Bangladeshi migrants in the UK (Gardner, 2002; Phillipson et al, 2003); to Italian migrants in Perth, Western Australia (Baldassar et al, 2007); and to members of the Turkish community living in Germany (Naegele, 2008). All of this movement reflects what Christine Ho (1991: 179) has described, in her research on Anglo-Trinidadians living in Los Angeles, as 'the concerted effort [of migrants] to sustain these connections across time and geography'.

In their study of Jamaican migrants, Bauer and Thompson (2006: 210–11) make the point that the possibilities for keeping in touch have greatly increased over the past decade: 'Cheaper flights have encouraged more frequent visits to distant kin. Some older women have become regular fliers visiting children and grandchildren [and] another interesting and apparently growing phenomenon is the transnational family reunion'. Wilding (2006) highlights the role of different forms of information and communication technology (ICT) – notably email – in maintaining contact across national boundaries. He suggests that:

> The use of ICTs is important for some transnational families in constructing or imagining a 'connected relationship', and enabling them to overlook their physical separation by time and space – even if only temporarily ... As a result of the instantaneity of e-mail communication, and possibly as a function of its frequently prosaic context, migrants in particular felt much more closely connected to their kin in their home country. (Wilding, 2006: 132)

The ties sustained between migrants and their homeland vary, however, in terms of the support provided, the regularity of return visits, and the likelihood of older relatives themselves visiting the second homeland. The next section of this chapter considers the research evidence on these aspects, drawing out the significance of care from a transnational perspective.

Migration, transnational communities and older people

In general terms, studies of older people have tended to focus on care delivered within defined communities and localities. Indeed, an unspoken assumption in the literature is that 'proper care' is that which is available close by or within the immediate vicinity of the older person. In contrast, research on transnational communities highlights the possibilities of sustaining support across considerable geographical distances. Baldassar (2007: 276), for example, provides: '... a critique of the preoccupation and assumption in the gerontology literature that care-giving requires proximity'. She goes on to note that: 'Empirically, the general preoccupation with geographic proximity means that very little research has been done on the relationships between ageing parents and adult children who live at a distance ... with the result that transnational practices of care have remained largely invisible or assumed to be unfeasible' (Baldassar (2007:276). Against this, if we recognise the different dimensions associated with care and support – practical, financial, personal, emotional and moral – then distinctive possibilities emerge for maintaining a caring relationship of one kind or another across national boundaries.

The research literature is only beginning to document the variety of supportive ties maintained by migrants, these reflecting the influence of cultural, economic and socio-legal factors that influence international migration. Baldassar (2007) makes the point that the capacity of migrants to assist relatives in their first homeland will reflect the economic resources at their disposal. But beyond this, it is also the case that:

> ... having the resources to participate does not necessarily mean that an individual will actively engage in transnational care-giving. The decision to exchange care, how and when, is also informed by the *negotiated commitments* that develop out of family histories and personal relationships within families ... Further, the particular practices of transnational care-giving are also influenced by a sense of obligation (felt need) to provide care, a notion that is closely bound up in cultural constructions of duty and social roles and responsibilities. (Baldassar, 2007: 280, emphasis in original; see further Chapter One)

Phillipson et al (2003) studied 100 first-generation Bangladeshi women aged between 35 and 55 living in Tower Hamlets, London. The majority of the women (71%) still had a mother alive – in most cases living in Bangladesh. Many of these respondents talked of the pressure – given their own difficult financial circumstances – to provide help to their mothers:

> I occasionally send some money. My heart can't bear it ... I always wonder if they are going without: 'Are they eating properly? What are they eating?' If I hear they are ill I don't know what to do. I don't have much to give myself. If only I could speak the language [English] I could work. Then I could open the letters from Bangladesh with a light heart, and write back to them and make them happy. Even if I do write to them they are upset – if you don't give them money they don't like you. (Phillipson et al, 2003: 55–6)

Others continue to maintain some support, in particular to their mothers:

> 'If we can give a bit of money to help with medicines ... Sometimes we send money over for her medication or so that they can buy her nice food.'
> 'Sometimes I would send a little money to her.'
> 'I send money as often as I can.' (Phillipson et al, 2003: 55–6)

Burholt (2004) examined the contacts maintained by first-generation south Asian migrants aged 55 and over living in Birmingham. Her study looked at the experiences of Gujaratis, Punjabis and Sylhetis in maintaining contact with children, siblings and other relatives living abroad. The research demonstrated important differences between the ethnic groups both in the type of contact and the links maintained between different family members. An important finding was that all the groups were more likely to visit siblings or relatives than children.

The findings indicated that contacts between extended family members seemed to be sustained in a way equivalent to those in the immediate family. Burholt (2004: 823) makes the point here that siblings in particular share a long history of intimate family experiences and that this relationship may become stronger in later life: 'Siblings and other extended family members, in the last years of life, are among the very few who have memories of their own parents and childhood ... the maintenance of these ties may encompass personal reminiscence in addition to the "reinforcement of a national identity abroad".'

Baldassar found that among first-generation Italian migrants to Australia the sense of duty to provide care for parents in their old age, far from being diminished by migration, was often intensified through their decision to remain permanently in their new homeland:

> These migrants followed a tradition of sending remittances to their parents in Italy that extends back to the date of their arrival. Financial assistance invariably flowed from migrant to homeland although other forms of care, such as emotional and practical support, were more reciprocal. They maintained contact initially through letters and more recently have begun to 'employ' their children and grandchildren to facilitate the exchange of information through e-mail, a practice that has significantly increased the involvement of the second and subsequent generations in transnational care-giving relationships. (Baldassar, 2007: 287)

Albanian migrants also maintain various forms of contact with relatives back home:

> Besides remittances, children are regularly in touch with their families by mobile phone. Every interviewee mentioned that their children spoke to them at least once a week, but the duration and frequency of the calls depended on the economic situation of the children since it was they who called. If the parents needed to speak to the children urgently, they made a brief call, and the son or daughter called back. Visits demonstrated even more that children cared for their parents, and also that they were successful migrants ... however, such visits may be blocked or limited by the migrant's 'illegal' status and by the cost of the trip. Visits by fellow-migrants are also part of the care, particularly when the children cannot visit themselves. (King and Vullnetari, 2004: 802)

Help and support is not, however, a one-way process from migrant in the second homeland to older person in the first homeland. Intergenerational ties will have been crucial, in many cases, in assisting the passage of the migrant to their destination – through help with the cost of emigration, advice and assistance, and, in some cases, care of dependent children until the migrant is settled in their new country. Bauer and Thompson (2006) highlight this point in their study of Jamaican families, where grandmothers have typically played a major role in caring for a child while mothers migrate in search of work (see also Goulborne, 1999). Grandparent emigration is another dimension to transnational communities, with grandparents in some cases moving abroad to provide help with childcare, thus freeing the mother to seek employment (King and Vullnetari, 2006). Some relatives may even shuttle between countries, in a restless search to maintain links with a now-divided family:

> She [respondent's mother] lived between this country [UK] and Bangladesh. She would go to Bangladesh because she missed my brother's children, but when she was back there she would miss us and come back. And when she came back she would start missing them and want to go back again. She didn't have peace in either country. While she was there she missed us, but she couldn't stay a year here before wanting to go back. She died in this country, but we sent her body back to Bangladesh. (Respondent in Phillipson et al, 2003: 56)

Transnational communities: the pressure of migration

Thompson and Bauer (2001) point to the sources of 'pain' on the one side, and 'resilience' on the other, associated with migration. The former has been reported both by those who leave and by those left behind. Bangladeshi women, often still in their teens when they migrated, commented in the study by Phillipson et al as follows:

> 'How could I feel? I left all my family behind – my mother, my father, my brothers. It felt bad. But I came. I couldn't really not come [to the UK] could I? My husband was here. I worried a lot for my family ... I missed them.'
> 'I felt very lonely. Anyone would feel like that if they went to a new country wouldn't they? I couldn't speak the language and I couldn't understand anyone around me when I went out.'
> 'When I went out it felt strange because I couldn't make sense of anything around me. I couldn't understand anything anyone said.' (Phillipson et al, 2003: 19)

Bauer and Thompson, from their study of Jamaican migrants, suggest that there is:

> ... a kind of grief intrinsic in migration itself, even when made in a spirit of betterment. Some migrants for years continued to feel a general sense of loss, which they expressed in terms of feeling

physically isolated. Migrant women were particularly likely to feel the absence of family and close local community at times of child birth, but sometimes men spoke of similar feelings of loss. (Bauer and Thompson, 2006: 5)

Baldassar (2007) suggests, however, that such feelings will vary across different groups, reflecting factors such as whether the individual comes from earlier or later cohorts of migrants and different stage of the family lifecycle. She studied three cohorts of migrants from Italy to Perth (Western Australia) who left respectively in the 1950s and 1960s, in the 1970s and 1980s, and in the 1990s. It was the intermediate group, who had migrated in the 1970s and 1980s, and who were now mostly in their 50s, who were experiencing the greatest difficulties in supporting parents in their first homeland:

> [This group] expressed the greatest concerns for ageing parents and providing care from a distance. Many have parents who can no longer speak on the phone due to dementia or who can no longer write due to disability ... Even those parents who are in good health consider visiting Perth too hazardous or are busy caring for an ailing spouse. This state of affairs generally results in this group being engaged in more intense 'distant thinking' and more frequent visits than the post-war cohort, whose parents are now deceased. Women, in particular, struggle with feelings of guilt about their inability to provide more support for their parents and to their siblings who are caring for parents. (Baldassar, 2007: 290)

Those left behind – especially older people – are likely to be affected by the departure of children in a variety of ways. Vullnetari and King's account of the impact of the migration of young people from Albania, though possibly an extreme case, highlights some of the issues:

> Our field data clearly demonstrate that one of the most distressing aspects of Albania's experience of the quasi-forced migration of such a large share of the young-adult cohorts is that older people have been denied the right to be *care givers*, especially to their grandchildren. All the interviewees who had children broke down in tears as they spoke of how much they missed being with them ... Other interviewees broadened the discussion about denied grandparenting to a linguistic and cultural dimension, counterbalancing the economic benefits of migration against the human price that has to be paid. (Vullnetari and King, 2008: 153-4)

Moreover, we know little about those migrants (invariably women) who may have experienced the forced rather than negotiated dimension to transnational care.

One of Gardner's migrant women in Tower Hamlets reported how she stayed with her in-laws while her husband had a family with an English woman in Britain:

> Earlier in the narrative she has mentioned that her husband married her so that his parents would have someone to care for them in Bangladesh. Now in her late thirties, she has been in the UK for two years ... As she tells us, she was 'sent for' by her husband after he became sick and his English wife left him. Their only child, a son, was taken to Britain by his father when he was nine; when she arrived in this country she had not seen him for five years. The anger she feels at her husband and his relatives is plain, even as she wraps her narrative in the rhetoric of duty. (in Gardner, 2002: 124)

But equally, there is often a sense of pride and achievement among migrants who have dealt with significant crises and difficulties in their lives. A respondent in Peggy Levitt's (2001: 102) study of migrants from the Dominican Republic to Los Angeles comments: 'The woman that migrates develops in many ways. She has to learn how to live alone, to do everything, and not to ask for anything.' And a Bangladeshi migrant in the study by Phillipson et al commented:

> How can you not change coming to a different country? You [to the interviewer] were born in this country. Why don't you go and live in Bangladesh for a few years? Wouldn't you become braver and more confident that you went and lived in another country ... that you coped? You have to have that courage ... that you have come to a new country. You don't have anyone here, so you have to be everything for yourself. You have to get on with things. (in Phillipson et al, 2003: 46)

Conclusion

The increasing importance of migration and mobility is now raising substantial questions for research, especially in respect of the political economy of informal and formal care (Torres, 2006). By way of conclusion, this point might be illustrated in three ways: first, the processes associated with migration raise the possibilities of new forms of ageism affecting older people in the 21st century. Older migrants in particular may represent an 'urban underclass', marginalised from key support services as well as dominant social and cultural institutions. This much is identified in the review by Warnes et al (2004: 318), which examined the position of older migrants across a number of European countries. The authors confirmed the extent to which gaps in social policy were leading to social exclusion as well as failure to respond to social and health care needs. Common problems were summarised as: '... inadequate guidance on the prevalent problems and unmet needs, and too little sharing of experience especially in approaches to the development of feasible and effective services'. The authors go on to note that:

> Many studies report not only the absence of interpreter services in health and welfare agencies and facilities, but also the unsympathetic reactions of 'front-line' staff, a consequence of the lack of training and of consciousness-raising by employers ... Researchers and academics could do more to assist managers and clinicians gain an understanding of how new services are successfully developed. (Warnes et al, 2004: 318)

Second, international migrants – viewed from another angle – are an important source of formal care for older people. Buchan et al (2005: 6) note that over the period 2000–04, overseas countries, on average, contributed about 45% of the annual number of new entrants to nursing in the UK. Migrant workers also play a key role in the area of social care, with foreign-born workers making up around 20% of the social care labour force in many regions, and over 70% in inner London (Economic and Social Research Council, 2009: 27). Such developments raise issues about the effect of these workers within care settings, both in terms of the quality of the work conditions they experience (eg in respect of pay and training) and the quality of care provided to older people. In the UK context, there has been some research addressing, for example, issues about the integration of migrant nurses within the National Health Service (Winkelmann-Gleed and Seely, 2005), as well as the impact of racism on different health care groups (Kyriakides and Virdee, 2003). Systematic study of these and related issues has, however, yet to be carried out. In particular, we need to know much more about the type of discrimination that may be experienced by overseas health and social care workers and the effect on the nature of care provided within hospitals, nursing homes and other settings (Phillipson, 2007).

Third, transnational communities bring major issues for social policy with the development of groups holding together care tasks or financial responsibilities that may be strung across continents. Cross-cultural social networks will continue to thrive, sustained through the expanded possibilities introduced by new technology (Vertovec, 2001). The key issue, however, is the extent to which these additional elements of citizenship are given due acknowledgement in the countries to which people migrate (Ackers and Dwyer, 2002). The argument here is that without such recognition new forms of social exclusion may appear and full participation in society may be compromised. Transnational communities do in fact promote social inclusion in a variety of ways – through generating new forms of social capital, through remittances, through paid and unpaid labour and through the maintenance of strong social ties. All of these aspects may be highly positive for older migrants, especially in a context where the welfare state is withdrawing from significant areas of responsibility. Greater understanding of the meaning of new forms of community is both an important challenge for social policy and a major issue for research into ageing to address.

NINE

Changing times: older people and family ties

The concerns of this book have focused on the character of family solidarities in later life at the beginning of the 21st century. For many years, there have been arguments that 'the family' is, in some global yet ill-defined way, no longer as supportive or as caring as it once was, especially with respect to later life relationships. This is part of a much wider discourse that perceives contemporary social formations as fostering greater individualisation at the expense of family and community commitment. According to those who subscribe to such a perspective, family ties have become attenuated, with people no longer having an unequivocal sense of kinship obligation and responsibility. Historians have, of course, challenged the view of past family relationships implicit in this model, arguing in particular that the material and demographic circumstances of previous social eras render such romanticised images suspect (see, for example, Gillis, 1997, as well as the discussion in Chapter Two above). Nonetheless, many of the changes associated with late modernity, including the growth of individualisation and the demographic shifts discussed in Chapter One, have given credence to a contemporary perception of family relationships becoming less significant in personal life than they were (Allan, 2008).

Our argument is certainly not that older people's family experiences have somehow remained static. How could this be with so much change occurring in the organisation of family life? But we do not accept that the family solidarities that older people sustain are now of little social or personal moment. Rather our argument is that there have been significant changes, but that these changes embody increasing diversity and complexity in the patterning of older people's family relationships rather than declining importance. As a result, there is greater variety in the circumstances structuring individual relationships within people's family networks. Because the lifecourse, in terms of both its family and non-family aspects, has become somewhat less certain and more varied, so too the family relationships within individuals' personal networks are liable to be more diverse and more open to change.

As a consequence, in the language drawn on earlier in the book, the negotiations that occur within family relationships across time are likely to be more complicated than in the past when there was greater stability in family formations. Established family practices are always open to shifts, especially as those involved alter their family status through marriage, parenting and other lifecourse changes. However, in contemporary family life, family practices are inherently that much more volatile in response to the reduced predictability of the lifecourse. And, as we have emphasised, what are important are not just the changes in the circumstances of the individuals directly involved in a particular relationship, but more the effects of the constellation of changes that occur across a family network.

To illustrate this, we want to present a brief cameo from a study of stepfamily kinship that one of us was involved in (see Allan et al, 2008). The cameo concerns Beryl, a woman in her late 60s, who was interviewed as part of that study.

Beryl's family

Beryl and Ralph had been married for nearly 50 years at the time of the interview. They had three sons, all them in their early to mid-40s, Jeff, Mike and Colin. Some 10 years before the interview, Beryl's family had been highly conventional. Her three sons were all married and all had children. By the time of the interview, however, two of her sons, Mike and Colin, had divorced and re-partnered with significant consequences for Beryl's family relationships.

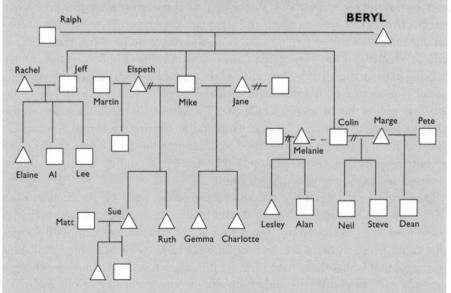

Mike had been married to Elspeth. They had two daughters, Sue, 22, and Ruth, 19 at the time of the interview. Mike had left Elspeth to live with Jane when the girls were 13 and 10. This caused a good deal of conflict within their families. Not only was Jane, like Mike, married, but all the families involved, including Jane's, belonged to the same church. Since then Elspeth had moved to a town some 40 miles away, remarried and had a son. Mike and Jane had also had two daughters, Gemma and Charlotte. Both Sue and Ruth had lived with their mother, though Sue left home at 16 after a series of arguments. As a result, Sue spent two years living with Beryl and Ralph. In this time she met Matt, whom she married. They now have two young children, Beryl's great-grandchildren. Colin, Beryl's third son, had been married to Marge. She left him to live with Pete when their two boys, Neil and Steve, now 16 and 13, were 5 and 3. Marge and Pete now have a son, Dean, aged 9. Neil and Steve both live with Marge, Pete and Dean. For most of the last 10 years Colin has cohabited with Melanie, who has two children, Lesley, 15, and Alan, 11, from a previous marriage.

Thus in the 10 years before the interview, Beryl's family circumstances had changed quite dramatically in ways that were not of her choosing. She was particularly upset that her relationships with some of her grandchildren had been so disrupted. However she continued to work at sustaining these relationships, albeit unsuccessfully at times. She, and Ralph, have close ties to Jeff's three children who live nearby, as well as to their mother Rachel (Beryl and Ralph's daughter-in-law). Beryl now also sees Mike, Jane and their two children regularly. Mike's separation from Elspeth and his re-partnering with Jane resulted in a high degree of antagonism. Beryl, like Mike, no longer has any relationship with Elspeth, a situation she regrets but sees as largely inevitable. Sue and Ruth's relationship with Mike, and consequently with Beryl, has been shaped by this conflict. Sue had little to do with her mother after leaving home, but has renewed contact since the birth of her first child. This has meant that she now sees little of her father, Mike, though she still sees Beryl and Ralph. Ruth, Sue's sister, now has no contact at all with Mike, Jane and her half-sisters, or with Beryl and Ralph. Beryl is upset by this, describing Ruth as 'rather special' to her and hopes the situation will change in the future. She sends Ruth presents and writes letters in an attempt to 'keep the door open'.

Beryl's grandsons, Neil and Steve, live locally. They stayed regularly with Beryl and Ralph for weekends after their parents, Colin and Marge, separated. Neil continues to be highly involved with his grandparents, often coming round to see them. Steve, however, now has very little to do with them. He has also 'suddenly' stopped visiting his father, Colin. Again Beryl hopes this will change. Against Ralph's wishes, she continues to send Steve presents and makes sure that he knows through Neil that he would always be welcome if he wanted to come to see them.

Beryl's story is instructive in a number of ways. There are four matters that are of particular relevance. The first concerns the demographic and generational shifts that have been occurring in families. The 50-year stability of Beryl's marriage contrasts noticeably with the quite different patterns of partnership formation and dissolution of the next generation. As a result of such changes family relationships and family histories have become more complex than they were. To draw on the common vernacular, people tend now to have to cope with more family 'baggage' than they did in the mid-20th century. Importantly, while much of the change that has taken place has had a more direct effect on earlier phases of the lifecourse, it nonetheless patterns the family experiences of older people, both directly and indirectly. As Beryl's story illustrates, increases in divorce, lone-parent families and cohabitation among younger cohorts have clear consequences for the organisation of intergenerational family relationships. Moreover, these sorts of demographic shift, which began in the mid-1970s (Allan and Crow, 2001), have now been occurring for a sufficiently long time to incorporate the generation currently entering older age. A good number of first-generation baby boomers – those born in the late 1940s – who are now reaching retirement age experienced some of these demographic trends at first hand (Leach et al, 2008).

The second issue that Beryl's account illustrates concerns the impact of family networks and the importance of seeing relational development as more than simply dyadic. Because individual family relationships are part of a broader family network, they are inevitably influenced, directly and indirectly, and over time, by the other ties that make up that network. Beryl's narrative illustrates this very clearly. The consequences of her sons' divorces and re-partnering had repercussions on Beryl's relationships with them, with their ex-spouses and with her grandchildren. In the process the constitution of what Beryl saw as 'her family' was altered. Over a 10-year period the family she had assumed was 'settled' had been highly disrupted. As well as creating worry about her sons' welfare, this also led to continuing concerns over the realignment of many of her other most important family relationships. Obvious though this might be, it can nonetheless sometimes be forgotten in discussions of later life family relationships.

Third, there is the issue of relational negotiation. As discussed in Chapter One, rather than simply following narrowly framed normative guidelines, individuals construct their family relationships through their interactions. In other words, family ties are negotiated between those involved, with their consequent structuring emerging across time as a result of their interactional histories. Beryl's account of her efforts to sustain active relationships with her grandchildren provides a good illustration of such processes of family negotiation. As noted, Beryl had a strong family orientation and had no desire to lose contact with any of her grandchildren. She wanted to be part of their lives and for them to be part of hers. As discussed above, she made concerted efforts to repair those relationships that had been damaged as a result of the divorce dynamics, sometimes successfully, sometimes not. Equally, it can be recognised that Beryl was only one of the players in these negotiations, in line with Finch and Mason's (1993) arguments. The state of her grandchildren's relationships with their parents patterned their involvement with Beryl. Note too the diversity there is in Beryl's relationships with her grandchildren. In effect, the diversity in her sons' partnership histories results in Beryl having far more diverse relationships with her grandchildren than otherwise would seem likely.

Fourth, Beryl's narrative of the changes in her family relationships over the last 10 years indicates the centrality of family within her life. There are many elements within her self-identity but her role as wife, mother and grandmother are evidently quite central to her sense of self. Beryl's commitment to these relationships was not always reciprocated in the fashion she wanted, though the dynamics of this are complex and appear to result predominantly from conflicting family pressures. Nonetheless, notwithstanding the changes there have been in Beryl's family network in the 10 years before the interview, there is no indication of any reduction in the centrality of family relationships to her. These relationships may no longer be taken for granted; they are more complex and more diverse than they were. But they remain core to Beryl's personal and social identity.

Family solidarity and change

In a number of ways Beryl's story captures what this book has been about. It reflects the rapid changes there have been in family constellations in recent years and highlights processes inherent in the 'doing' of family. It is essentially a modern story of family relationships in which individuals need to come to terms with higher levels of diversity and flux that undermine once-conventional assumptions about stability. And yet, at the same time, continuities in family practice and family ideology are evident. This is especially so with regard to intergenerational solidarities. Despite the problems that Beryl experiences in sustaining ties with some of her grandchildren, the continuing importance of intergenerational solidarities is evident.

Here we return to Bengtson's (2001) emphasis on the importance of researchers seeing families through a multigenerational lens. Whether or not one agrees with Bengtson's argument that less stable forms of marriage and partnership mean that descendent kinship is replacing the nuclear family as the key structural element in early 21st-century family life, it is certainly difficult to argue that intergenerational ties are of little consequence. For many they provide a major source of reliable practical and emotional support and continue to be central in their personal and social identities. Of course, increases in separation, divorce and lone-mother births have resulted in some fathers having comparatively little relationship with some of their children. But even allowing for this, intergenerational family relationships still lie at the heart of most people's understandings of 'family'.

As we consider the next 30 years or so, it seems to us unlikely that Bengtson's thesis of the significance of multigenerational family bonds will be significantly undermined. Certainly there seems little reason to believe that older generations will become less attached, less concerned or even less involved with younger generations than they are now. Dominant public discourses about the ageing population are that as a society we need to prepare for the burdens of old age. These include economic dependence on a proportionately reduced employed population and increased demand for formal and informal health and social support. What these discourses tend to ignore is the increasing numbers of active and healthy older people that there will be in society. Not only will these people resist any drift into inactivity and dependence; they will, like many currently retired people, adopt new modes of retired lifestyle that entail participation in a range of social relationships.

For many, family ties will form a part – but only a part – of the emergent lifestyle. As above, such ties will not represent a dependency on the part of the older cohort but an interdependency in which they are providing, as well as receiving, mundane support. It is worth remembering here that some 20% of children under the age of 16 are looked after by grandparents during the daytime (Clarke and Cairns, 2001). Not all of these grandparents are of retirement age, but this nonetheless is indicative of routine generational involvement and exchange. Though it did not figure in Beryl's story above, we should also note the part played by some sibling ties in later life. As we discussed in Chapter Five, brother and sister relationships vary widely, with some being socially distant but others very close. In later life, there is some evidence that sibling ties can become stronger, offering companionship and validating biographical constructions of the past.

Conclusion

In conclusion, we want to re-emphasise the importance of taking a lifecourse perspective for understanding the family experiences of older people, however the category 'older' is defined. Along with the concepts of family practice, negotiation and diversity, this has been a prominent theme throughout this book. Our argument is simple: family relationships are developmental and emergent. The relationships themselves alter over time as people's proclivities and their material and social circumstances change. But equally, people's relationships alter as the circumstances of others in their familial and wider networks change. To understand this requires a lifecourse perspective; that is, a perspective that focuses on change and recognises that an understanding of the present benefits from an appreciation of the past. This is even more true in contemporary times, given the diversity of family relationships and networks. As we have seen from the cameo of Beryl's family experiences, the formation and dissolution of partnerships is having an impact on family matters well beyond those most intimately concerned. And, of course, in the future the numbers of people whose own biographies encompass changed partnerships and complex generational relationships will increase. In the light of these emerging patterns, a lifecourse perspective on older people's family relationships is likely to become even more imperative than it is now.

Throughout this book we have explored how people's constructions of family relationships in later life have been changing. A number of themes have been important in this. First, we have emphasised how crucial it is within family analysis to focus on the lifecourse. People's relational experiences have a past as well as a present; they are not forged from a blank canvas. Understanding how relationships have come to be structured in the ways that they are requires knowledge of their histories. It also requires knowledge of the range of events external to any specific relationships that, to a greater or lesser extent, provide the context in which family relationships are worked out. A lifecourse perspective allows family relationships to be interpreted historically and contextually, the relationships within families being seen as consequent on, but in turn also constitutive of, the interweaving of people's different experiences over time.

The external issues that help shape family relationships across the lifecourse include the major divisions that affect social and economic experiences more broadly. These include class and gender, in particular, but also ethnicity, sexuality and age itself. Such factors as these act across the lifecourse; their patterning in earlier life phases may not determine lifestyles in older age but they are certainly of consequence in shaping the opportunities and constraints that people experience. Thus, the material circumstances of later life are heavily influenced by people's economic and occupational histories, that is, their lifetime class location. In particular, the consequences of access to different pension arrangements affect very directly the experiences of older people. In recent years, many who had middle-class occupations have benefited from generous pension provisions (even allowing for some of the pension fund shifts over the last 20 years), certainly in comparison with earlier generations. Yet even though there has been a wider distribution of occupational pension schemes, many who were employed in lower-class occupations have later life pensions that leave them on the fringes of poverty.

Similarly gender continues to influence lifestyles in later life, not just through the construction of masculinities and femininities per se, but also as a result of occupational and domestic differentiation. While many women have benefited from the increased pension coverage of the later 20th century, their access to adequate pensions in their own right in later life continues to lag behind that of men (Ginn, 2003). Widows are particularly likely to have limited resources for the remaining years of their lives. Equally, as discussed in Chapter Eight, many ethnic minority older people have very limited resources in their later years. Aspects of class, ethnic discrimination and migration histories interact to result in curtailed access to pension provision other than that provided by the state. And, as above, gender also plays its part here with ethnic minority older women being particularly likely to experience poverty. In addition, many ethnic minority older people live in poor-quality housing and have limited access to other forms of welfare support (Phillipson et al, 2001).

Thus, class, gender, ethnicity and other such structural divisions are core in differentiating the experiences of later life, in large part, though not only, through their impact on older people's material circumstances. In turn, these differential opportunities and constraints influence the construction and negotiation − the doing − of family relationships in later life. This is the point we wish to end on: understanding family relationships in later life requires an understanding of biography, of how older people have come to be in the circumstances they are in, and how the opportunities open to them have been generated across their lifetime. In these ways a lifecourse perspective is essential.

References

Ackers, L. and Dwyer, P. (2002) *Senior citizenship: Retirement, migration and welfare,* Bristol: Policy Press.

Adams, R. and Blieszner, R. (eds) (1989) *Older adult friendship: Structure and process,* Newbury Park: Sage.

Adlersberg, M. and Thorne, S. (1992) 'Emerging from the chrysalis', *Journal of Gerontological Nursing,* 6, pp 4–8.

Alford-Cooper, F. (1998) *For keeps: Marriages that last a lifetime,* New York: M.E. Sharpe.

Allan, G. (1977) 'Sibling solidarity', *Journal of Marriage and the Family,* 39, pp 173–88.

Allan, G. (2008) 'Flexibility, friendship, and family', *Personal Relationships,* 15, pp 1–16.

Allan, G. and Crow, G. (2001) *Families, households and society,* Basingstoke: Palgrave.

Allan, G., Hawker, S. and Crow, G. (2003) 'Britain's changing families', in M. Coleman and L. Ganong (eds), *Handbook of contemporary families,* Thousand Oaks, CA: Sage, pp 302–16.

Allan, G., Hawker, S. and Crow, G. (2008) 'Kinship in stepfamilies', in J. Pryor (ed), *The international handbook of stepfamilies: Policy and practice in legal, research, and clinical environments,* Hoboken, NJ: Wiley and Sons, pp 323–44.

Allan, G., Hawker, S. and Crow, G. (forthcoming) *Stepfamilies,* London: Palgrave Macmillan.

Arber, S. and Attias-Donfut, C. (eds) (2000) *The myth of generational conflict,* London: Routledge.

Arber, S. and Ginn, J. (1991) *Gender and later life: A sociological analysis of resources and constraints,* London, Sage.

Arber, S., Davidson, K. and Ginn, J. (2003) 'Changing approaches to gender and later life', in S. Arber, K. Davidson and J. Ginn (eds), *Gender and ageing: Changing roles and relationships,* Maidenhead: Open University Press, pp 1–14.

Askham, J. (1995) 'The married lives of older women', in S. Arber and J. Ginn (eds), *Connecting gender and ageing: A sociological approach,* Buckingham: Open University Press, pp 87–98.

Askham, J., Ferring, D. and Lamura, G. (2007) 'Personal relationships in later life', in J. Bond, S. Peace, F. Dittman-Kohli and G. Westerhof (eds), *Ageing in society,* 3rd edn, London: Sage, pp 186–209.

Atchley, R. (1992) 'Retirement and marital satisfaction', in M. Szinocacz, D. Ekerdt and B. Vinick (eds), *Families and retirement,* Newbury Park, CA: Sage, pp 145–58.

Atchley, R. (1999) *Continuity and adaptation in aging: Creating positive experiences.* Baltimore: Johns Hopkins University Press.

Attias-Donfut, C. and Segalen, M. (2002) 'The construction of grandparenthood', *Current Sociology*, 50, pp 281–94.

Attias-Donfut, C. and Wolff, F.-C. (2000) 'The redistributive effects of generational transfers', in S. Arber and C. Attias-Donfut (eds), *The myth of generational conflict*, London: Routledge, pp 22–46.

Baars, J., Dannefer, D., Phillipson, C. and Walker, A. (eds) (2006) *Aging, globalization and inequality: The new critical gerontology*, Amityville, NY: Baywood Publishing Company, Inc.

Baldassar, L. (2007) 'Transnational families and aged care: The mobility of care and the migrancy of ageing', *Journal of Ethnic and Migration Studies*, 33, 2, pp 275–97.

Baldassar, L., Baldock, C. and Wilding, R. (2007) *Families caring across borders: Migration, ageing and transnational caregiving*, Basingstoke: Palgrave Macmillan.

Baltes, P. and Baltes, M. (eds) (1990) *Successful aging: Perspectives from the behavioral sciences*, Cambridge: Cambridge University Press.

Barnes, H. and Parry, J. (2004) 'Renegotiating identity and relationships: Men's and women's adjustment to retirement', *Ageing and Society*, 24, pp 213–33.

Basch, L., Schiller, N. and Blanc-Szanton, C. (1994) *Nations unbound: Transnational projects, post-colonial predicaments and de-territorialised nation-states*, Langhorne, PA: Gordon and Breach.

Bauer, E. and Thompson, P. (2006) *Jamaican hands across the Atlantic*, Kingston, Jamaica: Ian Randle Publishers.

Beck, U. (1992) *Risk society: Towards a new modernity*, London: Sage.

Bedford, V.H. (1997) 'Sibling relationships in middle adulthood and old age', in R.M. Blieszner and V.H. Bedford (eds), *Handbook on aging and the family*, Westport, CT: Praeger, pp 201–2.

Bedford, V.H. (1989) 'Ambivalence in adult sibling relationships', *Journal of Family Issues*, 10, pp 211–24.

Bell, C. (1968) *Middle class families*, London: Routledge and Kegan Paul.

Bengtson, V. (2001) 'Beyond the nuclear family: The increasing importance of multigenerational bonds', *Journal of Marriage and Family*, 63, pp 1–16.

Bengtson, V., Giarrusso, R., Mabry, B. and Silverstein, M. (2002) 'Solidarity, conflict and ambivalence: Complementary or competing perspectives on intergenerational relationships', *Journal of Marriage and Family*, 64, pp 568–76.

Bird, E. and West, J. (1987) 'Interrupted lives: A study of women returners', in P. Allatt, T. Keil, A. Bryman and B. Bytheway (eds), *Women and the life-cycle: Transitions and turning points*, Basingstoke: Macmillan, pp 178–91.

Blando, J.A. (2001) 'Twice hidden: Older gay and lesbian couples, friends, and intimacy', *Generations*, Summer, pp 87–9.

Bonvalet, C. and Ogg, J. (eds) (2007) *Measuring family support in Europe*, London: Southern Universities Press.

Borell, K. and Karlsson, S. (2003) 'Reconceptualising intimacy and ageing: Living apart together', in S. Arber, K. Davidson and J. Ginn (eds), *Gender and ageing: Changing roles and relationships*, Maidenhead: Open University Press, pp 47–62.

Bornat, J. (ed) (1996) *Reminiscence reviewed*, Buckingham: Open University Press.

Bradshaw, J., Stimson, C., Skinner, C. and Williams, J. (1999) *Absent fathers?*, London: Routledge.

Buchan, J., Jobanputra, R., Gough, P. and Hutt, R. (2005) *Internationally recruited nurses in London: Profile and implications for policy*, London: King's Fund Centre.

Budgeon , S. (2006) 'Friendship and formations of sociality in late modernity: The challenge of "post-traditional" intimacy', *Sociological Research Online*, 11, 3, at http://www.socresonline.org.uk/11/3/budgeon.html.

Burgoyne, J. and Clark, D. (1984) *Making a go of it*, London: Routledge and Kegan Paul.

Burholt, V. (2004) 'Transnationalism, economic transfers and families' ties: Intercontinental contacts of older Gujaratis, Punjabis and Sylhetis in Birmingham with families abroad', *Ethnic and Racial Studies*, 27, 5, pp 800–29.

Burholt, V. and Wenger, G.C. (1998) 'Differences over time in older people's relationships with children and siblings', *Ageing and Society*, 18, pp 537–62.

Butler, R.N. (1980) 'Life review: An interpretation of reminiscence in the aged', *Psychiatry*, 26, pp 65–76.

Cabinet Office (2008) 'Families in Britain: An evidence paper', at www.cabinetoffice.gov.uk/media/111945/families_in_britain.pdf.

Cahill, S. and South, K. (2002) 'Policy issues affecting lesbian, gay, bisexual and transgender people in retirement', *Generations*, Summer, pp 49–54.

Cahill, S., South, K. and Spade, J. (2000) *Outing age: Public policy issues affecting gay, lesbian, bisexual and transgender elders*, Washington, DC: National Gay and Lesbian Task Force Policy Institute.

Carrington, C. (1999) *No place like home: Relationships and family life among lesbians and gay men*, Chicago, IL: University of Chicago Press.

Chambers, P. (2005) *Older widows and the life course: Multiple narratives of hidden lives*, Aldershot: Ashgate.

Chambers, P. (2006) 'Brothers and sisters: Growing up and growing old, together and apart', Paper presented at the British Society of Gerontology Annual Conference, University of Wales Bangor.

Chambers, P. (2009) 'Age and ageing', in E. Denny and S. Earle (eds), *Sociology for Nurses*, Cambridge: Polity Press, pp 104–20.

Charles, N., Davies, C.A. and Harris, C. (2008) *Families in transition: Social change, family formation and kin relationships*, Bristol: The Policy Press.

Cherlin, A. (2004) 'The deinstitutionalization of American marriage', *Journal of Marriage and the Family*, 66, pp 848–61.

Cherlin, A. and Furstenberg, F. (1992) *The new American grandparent*, Cambridge, MA: Harvard University Press.

Cherlin, A. and Furstenberg, F. (1994) 'Stepfamilies in the United States: A reconsideration', *American Review of Sociology*, 20, pp 359–81.

Cicirelli, V.G. (1995) *Sibling relationships across the life span*, New York: Plenum Press.

Clarke, L. and Cairns, H. (2001) 'Grandparents and childcare: The research evidence', in B. Broad (ed), *Kinship care: The placement choice for children and young people*, Lyme Regis: Russell House Publishing, pp 11–20.

Clarke, L. and Roberts, C. (2004) 'The meaning of grandparenthood and its contribution to the quality of life of older people', in A. Walker and C. Hennessy (eds), *Growing older: Quality of life in old age*, Maidenhead: Open University Press, pp 188–208.

Clarke, L., Evandrou, M. and Warr, P. (2005) 'Family and economic roles', in A. Walker (ed), *Understanding quality of life in old age*, Maidenhead: Open University Press, pp 64–83.

Coleman, M., Ganong, L. and Cable, S.M. (1997) 'Beliefs about women's intergenerational family obligations to provide support before and after divorce and remarriage', *Journal of Marriage and the Family*, 59, pp 165–76.

Connidis, I. (1994) 'Sibling support in later life', *Journal of Gerontology*, 49, pp 309–17.

Connidis, I. (2001) *Family ties and aging,* Thousand Oaks, CA: Sage.

Connidis, I. and Campbell, L. (2001) 'Closeness, confiding and contact among siblings in mid-life and late-adulthood', in A. Walker, M. Manoogian-O'Dell, L. McGraw and D. White (eds), *Families in later life: Connections and transitions*, Thousand Oaks, CA: Pine Forge Press, pp 149–55.

Connidis, I. and McMullin, J. (2002) 'Ambivalence, family ties, and doing sociology', *Journal of Marriage and the Family*, 64, pp 594–601.

Coulthard, M. and Walker, A. (2002) *People's perceptions of their neighbourhoods and community involvement. Results from the social capital module of the general household survey, 2000*, London: The Stationery Office.

Cowgill, D. and Holmes, D. (eds) (1972) *Ageing and modernization*, New York: Appleton-Century-Crofts.

Crosnoe, R. and Elder, G. (2002) 'Life course transitions, the generational stake, and grandparent-grandchild relationships', *Journal of Marriage and the Family*, 64, pp 1089–96.

Daatland, S.O. and Herlofson, K. (2003) '"Lost solidarity" or "changed solidarity": A comparative European view of normative family solidarity', *Ageing and Society*, 23, pp 537–61.

Davidson, K. (1999) 'Gender, age and widowhood: How older widows and widowers differently realign their lives', unpublished PhD thesis, University of Surrey.

Davidson, K. (2001) 'Late life widowhood, selfishness and new partnership choices: A gendered perspective', *Ageing and Society*, 21, pp 297–317.

Davidson, K. (2004) 'Gender differences in new partnership choices and constraints for older widows and widowers', in K. Davidson and G. Fennell (eds), *Intimacy in later life*, New Brunswick, NJ: Transaction Publishers, pp 65–84.

Davidson, K., Daly, T. and Arber, S. (2003) 'Exploring the social worlds of older men', in S. Arber, K. Davidson and J. Ginn (eds), *Gender and ageing: Changing roles and relationships*, Maidenhead: Open University Press, pp 168–85.

De Jong Gierveld, J. (2004) 'The dilemma of re-partnering: considerations of older men and women entering new intimate relationships in later life', in K. Davidson and G. Fennell (eds), *Intimacy in later life*, New Brunswick, NJ: Transaction Publishers, pp 85–104.

De Jong Gierveld, J. and Peeters, A. (2003) 'The interweaving of repartnered older adults' lives with their children and siblings', *Ageing and Society*, 23, pp 187–206.

de Vries, B. (2007) 'LGBT couples in later life: A study in diversity', *Generations*, Fall, pp 18–23.

Dench, G. and Ogg, J. (2002) *Grandparenting in Britain*, London: Institute of Community Studies.

Department for Work and Pensions (2005) *Opportunity age: Volume 2, A social portrait of ageing in Britain*, at www.dwp.gov.uk/opportunity_age/.

Duck, S. (1999) *Relating to others*, 2nd edn, Buckingham: Open University Press.

Dunne, G. A. (1997) *Lesbian lifestyles: Women's work and the politics of sexuality*, London: Macmillan.

Dykstra, P. (2006) 'Off the beaten track: Childlessness and social integration in late life', *Research on Aging*, 28, pp 749–67.

Dykstra, P. and Hagestad, G. (2007) 'Roads less taken: Developing a nuanced view of older adults without children', *Journal of Family Issues*, 28, pp 1275–310.

English Longitudinal Study on Ageing, www.ifs.org.uk/elsa.

ESRC (Economic and Social Research Council) (2009) 'Social care: The role of migrant workers', *Britain in 2009*, Swindon: ESRC, p 27.

Estes, C. and Phillipson, C. (2002) 'The globalization of capital, the welfare state and old age policy', *International Journal of Health Services*, 32, pp 279–97.

Ferguson, N., Douglas, G., Lowe, N., Murch, M. and Robinson, M. (2004) *Grandparenting in divorced families*, Bristol: The Policy Press.

Finch, J. (1989) *Family obligations and social change*, Oxford: Blackwell.

Finch, J. (2007) 'Displaying families', *Sociology*, 41, pp 65–81.

Finch, J. and Mason, J. (1990) 'Divorce, remarriage and family obligations', *British Journal of Sociology*, 38, pp 219–46.

Finch, J. and Mason, J. (1993) *Negotiating family responsibilities*, London: Routledge.

Finch, J. and Summerfield, P. (1991) 'Social reconstruction and the emergence of companionate marriage, 1945–59', in J. Burgoyne and D. Clark (eds), *Marriage, domestic life and social change*, London: Routledge, pp 7–32.

Fischer, D.H. (1977) *Growing old in America*, Oxford: Oxford University Press.

Fokkema, T., Bekke, S. and Dykstra, P. (2008) *Solidarity between parents and their adult children in Europe*, Amsterdam: Netherlands Interdisciplinary Demographic Institute, KNAW Press.

Frankenberg, R. (1966) *Communities in Britain*, Harmondsworth: Penguin.

Gardner, K. (2002) *Age, narrative and migration*, Oxford: Berg.

Gauthier, A. (2002) 'The role of grandparents', *Current Sociology*, 50, pp 295–307.

George, V. and Wilding, P. (2002) *Globalization and human welfare*, London: Palgrave.

Gibson, D. (1996) 'Broken down by age and gender: "The problem" of older women', *Gender and Society*, 10, pp 443–8.

Giddens, A. (1992) *The transformation of intimacy*, Cambridge: Polity.

Giele, J.Z. and Elder, G.H. (1998) *Methods of life course research*, Thousand Oaks, CA: Sage.

Gillis, J.R. (1997) *A world of their own making*, Oxford: Oxford University Press.

Ginn, J. (2003) *Gender, pensions and the lifecourse*, Bristol: The Policy Press.

Godfrey. M., Townsend, J. and Denby, T. (2004) *Building a good life for older people in local communities: The experiences of ageing in time and place*, York: Joseph Rowntree Foundation.

Gold, D. (1987) 'Siblings in old age: Something special' *Canadian Journal on Aging*, 6, pp 199–215.

Gold, D. (1989) 'Sibling relationships in old age: A typology', *International Journal of Aging and Human Development*, 28, pp 37–51.

Goodman, C. and Silverstein, M. (2001) 'Grandmothers who parent their grandchildren: An exploratory study of close relations across three generations', *Journal of Family Issues*, 22, pp 557–78.

Gottman, J. (1994) *What predicts divorce?*, New Jersey: Erlbaum.

Goulborne, H. (1999) 'The transnational character of Caribbean kinship in Britain', in S. McRae (ed), *Changing Britain: Families and households in the 1990s*, Oxford: Oxford University Press, pp 176–98.

Grinwald, S. and Shabat, T. (1997) 'The invisible figure of the deceased spouse in remarriage', *Journal of Divorce and Remarriage*, 26, pp 105–13.

Grundy, E. (1999) 'Intergenerational perspectives on family and household change in mid- and later life in England and Wales', in S. McRae (ed), *Changing Britain: Families and households in the 1990s*, Oxford: Oxford University Press, pp 201–28.

Grundy, E. and Henretta, J. (2006) 'Between elderly parents and adult children: A new look at the intergenerational care provided by the "sandwich generation"', *Ageing and Society*, 26, pp 707–22.

Grundy, E., Murphy, M. and Shelton, N. (1999) 'Looking beyond the household: Intergenerational perspectives on living kin and contacts with kin in Great Britain', *Population Trends*, 97, pp 19–27.

Gulati, L. (1993) *In the absence of their men: The impact of male migration on women*, New Delhi: Sage.

Haber, C. and Gratton, B. (1994) *Old age and the search for security: An American social history*, Bloomington, IN: Indiana University Press.

Hagestad, G. (1986) 'The aging society as a context for family life', *Daedelus*, 115, pp 119–40.

Hagestad, G. and Herlofsen, K. (2007) 'Micro and macro perspectives on intergenerational relations and transfers in Europe', in *Report from United Nations Expert Group Meeting on Social and Economic Implications of Changing Population Age Structures,* New York: United Nations/Department of Economic and Social Affairs, pp 339–57, available at www.un.org/esa/population/meetings/Proceedings_EGM_Mex_2005/

Hall, C., Brown, A., Glesson, S. and Zinn, J. (2007) 'Older men's networks in Sydney, Australia', *Quality in Ageing: Policy, Practice and Research*, 8, pp 10–16.

Hanawalt, B. (1986) *The ties that bound*, Oxford: Oxford University Press.

Hareven, T. (1982) *Family time and industrial time*, Cambridge: Cambridge University Press.

Hawkins, D.N. and Booth, A. (2005) 'Unhappily ever after: Effects of long-term, low quality marriages on well-being', *Social Forces*, 84, pp 446–65.

Heaphy, B., Donovan, C. and Weeks, J. (1999) 'Sex, money and the kitchen sink: Power in same-sex couple relationships', in J. Seymour and P. Bagguley (eds), *Relating intimacies: Power and resistance*, Basingstoke: Macmillan, pp 222–45.

Heaphy, B., Yip, A. and Thompson, D. (2004) 'Ageing in a non-heterosexual context', *Ageing and Society*, 24, pp 881–902.

Held, D., McGrew, A., Goldblatt, D. and Perraton, J. (1999) *Global transformations*, Cambridge: Polity.

Hilpern, K. (2008) *Saturday Guardian* (Family section), 30 August.

Ho, C. (1991) *Salt-water trinnies: Afro-Trinidadian immigrant networks and non-assimilation in Los Angeles,* New York: AMS Press.

Hochschild, A. (1973) *The unexpected community*, Berkeley, CA: University of California Press.

Hochschild, A. (2000) 'Global care chains and emotional surplus value', in W. Hutton and A. Giddens (eds), *On the edge: Living with global capitalism*, London: Jonathan Cape, pp 130–46.

Hockey, J. and James, A. (2003) *Social identities across the life course*, Basingstoke: Palgrave Macmillan.

Hoff, A. and Tesch-Römer, C. (2007) 'Family relations and aging: Substantial changes since the middle of the last century?', in H.-W. Wahl, C. Tesch-Römer and A. Hoff (eds), *New dynamics in old age*, Amityville: Baywood Publishing Co, pp 65–84.

Holden, K. (2007) *The shadow of marriage: Singleness in England, 1914–1960*, Manchester: Manchester University Press.

Huyck, M. (2001) 'Romantic relationships in later life', *Generations*, 25, pp 9–17.

Jenkins, R. (1996) *Social identity*, London: Routledge.

Jerrome, D. (1981) 'The significance of friendship for women in later life', *Ageing and Society*, 1, pp 175–97.

Jerrome, D. (1990) 'Frailty and friendship', *Journal of Cross Cultural Gerontology*, 5, pp 51–64.

Jerrome, D. and Wenger, G.C. (1999) 'Change and stability in confidant relationships: Findings from the Bangor Longitudinal Study of Ageing', *Journal of Aging Studies*, 13, pp 269–94.

Johnson, M. (1978) 'That was your life', in V. Carver and P. Liddiard (eds), *An ageing population*, Sevenoaks: Hodder and Stoughton, pp 98–113.

Johnson, S.E. (1990) *Staying power: Long term lesbian couples*, Tallahassee: Naiad Press.

Kaslow, F. and Robison, J. (1996) 'Long-term satisfying marriages: Perceptions of contributing factors', *American Journal of Family Therapy*, 24, pp 153–70.

Kemp, C.L. (2005) 'Dimensions of grandparent–adult grandchild relationships: From family ties to intergenerational friendships', *Canadian Journal on Aging*, 24, pp 161–77.

Kertzer, D. (1995) 'Towards a historical demography of aging', in D. Kertzer and P. Laslett (eds), *Aging in the past*, Berkeley: University of California Press, pp 363–84.

Khanum, S.M. (1994) '"We just buy illness in exchange for hunger": Experiences of health care, health and illness among Bangladeshi women In Britain', unpublished PhD thesis, Keele University.

King, R. and Vullnetari, J. (2006) 'Orphan pensioners and migrating grandparents: The impact of mass migration on older people in rural Albania', *Ageing and Society*, 26, pp 783–816.

Kohli, M., Kundemünd, H., Motel, A. and Szydlik, M. (2000) 'Families apart: Intergenerational transfers in East and West Germany', in S. Arber and C. Attias-Donfut (eds), *The myth of generational conflict: The family and state in ageing societies*, London: Routledge, pp 88–99.

Kulik, L. (2000) 'Marital equality and the quality of long-term marriage in later life', *Ageing and Society*, 22, pp 459–81.

Kurdek, L.A. (1994) 'Conflict resolution styles in gay, lesbian and heterosexual nonparent and heterosexual parent couples', *Journal of Marriage and the Family*, 56, pp 705–22.

Kurdek, L.A. (1995) 'Assessing multiple determinants of relationship commitment in cohabiting gay, cohabiting lesbian, dating heterosexual and married heterosexual couples', *Family Relations*, 44, pp 261–6.

Kyriakides, C. and Virdee, S. (2003) 'Migrant labour, racism and the British National Health Service', *Ethnic Health*, 8, pp 283–305.

Laslett, P. (1977) *Family life and illicit love in earlier generations*, Cambridge: Cambridge University Press.

Laslett, P. (1984) 'The significance of the past in the study of ageing', *Ageing and Society*, 4, pp 379–89.

Lauer, R. and Lauer, J. (1990) 'The long-term marriage: Perceptions of stability and satisfaction', *International Journal of Aging and Human Development*, 31, pp 189–95.

Leach, R., Phillipson, C., Biggs, S. and Money, A.-M. (2008) 'Sociological perspectives on the baby boomers: An exploration of social change', *Quality in Ageing*, 9, pp 19–26.

Leonard, D. (1980) *Sex and generation*, London: Tavistock.

Levitt, P. (2001) *The transnational villagers*, Berkeley, CA: University of California Press.

Litwak, E. (1960) 'Occupational Mobility and extended family cohesion', *American Sociological Review*, 25, pp 9–21.

Lopata, H.Z. (1973) *Widowhood in an American city*, Cambridge, MA: Schenkman.

Lopata, H.Z. (1996) *Current widowhood: Myths and realities*, Newbury Park: Sage.

Lowenstein, A. (2007) 'Intergenerational solidarity: Strengthening economic and social ties', paper for UN Social Policy Division Expert Group Meeting, 23–25 October, United Nations Headquarters, New York.

Lowenstein, A. and Daatland, S.O. (2006) 'Filial norms and family support in a comparative cross-national context: Evidence from the OASIS study', *Ageing and Society*, 26, pp 203–24.

Lowenstein, A., Katz, R. and Gur-Yaish, N. (2007) 'Reciprocity in parent–child exchange and life satisfaction among the elderly: A cross national perspective', *Journal of Social Issues*, 63, pp 865–83.

Luscher, K. (2002) 'Intergenerational ambivalence: Further steps in theory and research', *Journal of Marriage and the Family*, 64, pp 585–93.

Mackey, R., Diemer, M. and O'Brien, B. (2004) 'Relational factors in understanding satisfaction in the lasting relationships of same-sex and heterosexual couples', *Journal of Homosexuality*, 47, pp 111–36.

Martin-Matthews, A. (1991) *Widowhood in later life*, Toronto: Butterworths.

Martin-Matthews, A. (1999) 'Widowhood', in S. Neysmith (ed), *Critical issues for social work practice and aging persons*, New York: Columbia University Press, pp 27–46.

Mason, J. (1987) 'A bed of roses? Women, marriage and inequality in later life', in P. Allatt, T. Keil, A. Bryman and B. Bytheway (eds), *Women and the life cycle: Transitions and turning-points*, Basingstoke: Macmillan, pp 90–106.

Mason, J., May, V. and Clarke, L. (2007) 'Ambivalence and the paradoxes of grandparenting', *Sociological Review*, 55, pp 687–706.

Massey, D. (2000) 'To study migration today, look to a parallel era', *Chronicle of Higher Education*, 18 August, pp B4–B5.

Matthews, S.H. (1979) *The social world of older women*, San Diego, CA: Sage.

Matthews, S.H. (2002) *Sisters and brothers/daughters and sons: Meeting the needs of old parents*, Bloomington, IN: Unlimited Publishing

Mauthner, M. (2002) *Sistering: Power and change in female relationships*, Basingstoke: Palgrave.

Mauthner, M. (2004) 'Distant lives, still voices: Sistering in family sociology', *Sociology*, 39, pp 623–42.

Means, R. (2007) 'The re-medicalisation of later life', in M. Bernard and T. Scharf (eds), *Critical perspectives on ageing societies*, Bristol: The Policy Press, pp 47–58.

Minkler, M. (1999) 'Intergenerational households headed by grandparents', *Journal of Aging Studies*, 13, pp 199–218.

Moore, A. and Stratton, D. (2001) *Resilient widowers: Older men speak for themselves*, New York: Springer.

Moore, A. and Stratton, D. (2004) 'The "current woman" in an older widower's life', in K. Davidson and G. Fennell (eds), *Intimacy in later life*, New Brunswick, NJ: Transaction Publishers, pp 121–42.

Morgan, D.H.J. (1996) *Family connections*, Cambridge: Polity.

Morgan, D.H.J. (1999) 'Risk and family practices: Accounting for change and fluidity in family life', in E. Silva and C. Smart (eds), *The new family?*, London: Sage, pp 13–30.

Mueller, M. and Elder, G. (2003) 'Family contingencies across the generations: Grandparent–grandchild relationships in holistic perspective', *Journal of Marriage and the Family*, 65, pp 404–17.

Murphy, M. (2004) 'Models of kinship from the developed world', in S. Harper (ed), *Families in ageing societies: A multi-disciplinary approach*, Oxford: Oxford University Press, pp 31–52.

Myers, S. and Booth, A. (1996) 'Men's retirement and marital quality', *Journal of Family Issues*, 17, pp 336–58.

Naegele, G. (2008) 'Age and migration in Germany: An overview with a special consideration of the Turkish population', paper presented to the 56th Annual Scientific Meeting of the Gerontological Society of America, Washington, DC.

Nazroo, J., Bajekal, M., Blane, D. and Grewal, I. (2004) 'Ethnic inequalities', in C. Hennessy and A. Walker (eds), *Growing older: Quality of life in old age*, Maidenhead: Open University Press, pp 35–59.

Nelson, M. (2006) 'Single mothers "do" family', *Journal of Marriage and the Family*, 68, pp 781–95.

O'Connor, P. (1992) *Friendships between women*, London: Harvester Wheatsheaf.

OASIS project website: http://oasis.haifa.ac.il.

Office of the Deputy Prime Minister (2006) *A sure start to later life: ending inequalities for older people*, Social Exclusion Unit Final Report, London: ODPM.

ONS (Office for National Statistics) (2001) Census, London: ONS, at www.ons.gov.uk/census/index.html.

ONS (2004) 'Social trends', London: ONS, at www.statistics.gov.uk/downloads/theme_social/Social_trends34/Social_Trends34.pdf.

ONS (2006) 'Birth statistics', London: ONS, at www.statistics.gov.uk/downloads/theme_population/FM1_34/FM1_no34_2005.pdf.

ONS (2007) 'Marriage, divorce and adoption statistics', London: ONS, at www.statistics.gov.uk/downloads/theme_population/FM2no32/FM2_32.pdf.

Ottaway, S. (2004) *The decline of life: old age in eighteenth-century England*, Cambridge: Cambridge University Press.

Parker, G. (1993) *With this body: Caring and disability in marriage*, Buckingham: Open University Press.

Parsons, T. (1959) 'The social structure of the family', in R. Anshen (ed) *The family: its function and destiny*, New York: Harper, pp 241–74.

Parsons, T. and Bales, R. (1955) *Family: Socialization and interaction process*, Glencoe, IL: The Free Press.

Patterson, C. (2000) 'Family relationships of lesbian and gay men', *Journal of Marriage and the Family*, 62, pp 1052–69.

Pelling, M. and Smith, R. (1991) *Life, death and the elderly*, London: Routledge.

Phillipson, C. (1998) *Reconstructing old age*, London: Sage.

Phillipson, C. (2007) 'Migration and health care for older people: Developing a global perspective (Commentary)', in K. W. Schaie and P. Uhlenberg (eds), *Social structures: Demographic change and the well-being of older persons*, New York, Springer Publishing, pp 158–69.

Phillipson, C. (2009) 'Pensions in crisis: Aging and inequality in a global age', in L. Rogne, C. Estes, B. Grossman, B. Hollister and E. Solway (eds), *Social insurance and social justice*, New York: Springer, pp 319–40.

Phillipson, C., Ahmed, N. and Latimer, J. (2003) *Women in between: A study of the experiences of Bangladeshi women living in Tower Hamlets*, Bristol: The Policy Press.

Phillipson, C., Bernard, M., Phillips, J. and Ogg, J. (2001) *The family and community life of older people*, London: Routledge.

Porche, M. and Purvin, D. (2008) '"Never in our lifetime": Legal marriage for same-sex couples in long-term relationships', *Family Relations*, 57, pp 144–59.

Porter, E. J. (1995) 'The life world of older widows: The context of the lived experience', *Journal of Women and Aging*, 7, pp 31–46.

Portes, A. and Bach, R. (1985) *Latin journey: Cuban and Mexican immigrants in the United States*, Berkeley, CA: University of California Press.

Price, E. (2008) 'Pride or prejudice? Gay men, lesbians and dementia', *British Journal of Social Work*, 38, pp 1337–52.

Ray, M. (2000) 'Older women, long-term marriage and care', in M. Bernard, J. Phillips, L. Machin and V. Harding-Davies (eds), *Women ageing: Changing identities, challenging myths*, Routledge: London, pp 148–67.

Ray, M. (2006) 'Informal care in the context of long-term marriage: The challenge to practice', *Practice*, 18, pp 129–42.

Riley, M. (1973) 'Aging and cohort succession: Interpretations and misinterpretations', *Public Opinion Quarterly*, 37, pp 35–49.

Roberts, E. (1998) *Women and families 1940–70*, London: Blackwell.

Robin, J. (1984) 'Family care of the elderly in a nineteenth century Devonshire parish', *Ageing and Society*, 4, pp 505–16.

Rosenfeld, D. (1999) 'Identity work among lesbian and gay elderly', *Journal of Ageing Studies*, 13, pp 121–45.

Rosenmayr, L. and Kockeis, E. (1963) 'Propositions for a sociological theory of ageing and the family', *International Social Science Journal*, 15, pp 410–26.

Rosenthal, C. and Gladstone, J. (2000) *Grandparenthood in Canada*, Ottawa: Vanier Institute of the Family.

Ross, M. and Milgram, J. (1982) 'Important variables in adult sibling relationships: A qualitative study', in M. Lamb and B. Sutton-Smith (eds), *Sibling relationships: Their nature and significance across the life-span*, Hillsdale, NJ: Lawrence Erlbaum, pp 225–49.

Rosser, C. and Harris, C.C. (1965) *The family and social change*, London: Routledge and Kegan Paul.

Rowe, D. (2007) *My dearest enemy, my dangerous friend: Making and breaking sibling bonds*, London: Routledge.

Ruth, J.-E. and Oberg, P. (1995) 'Ways of life: Old age in a life history perspective', in J. Birren, G.M. Kenyon, J.-E. Ruth, J.J.F. Schroots and T. Svenson (eds), *Explorations in adult development*, New York: Springer, pp 167–86.

Scharf, T., Phillipson, C., Smith, A. and Kingston, P. (2002) *Growing older in socially deprived areas: Social exclusion in later life*, London: Help the Aged.

Scharf, T., Phillipson, C. and Smith, A. (2004) 'Poverty and social exclusion: experiences of older people from black and minority ethnic groups in deprived areas', in A. Walker with S. Northmore (eds), *Growing older in a black and ethnic minority group*, London: Age Concern, pp 33–44.

Scharf, T., Phillipson, C. and Smith, A (2005) 'Multiple exclusion and quality of life amongst excluded older people', in *Disadvantaged neighbourhoods*, London: Social Exclusion Unit, Office of the Deputy Prime Minister.

Schneider, D. (1968) *American kinship: A cultural account*, Englewood Cliffs, NJ: Prentice-Hall.

Shanas, E., Townsend, P., Wedderburn, D., Friis, H., Milhoi, P. and Stehouwer, J. (1968) *Old people in three industrial societies*, London: Routledge and Kegan Paul.

Shardlow, S., Johnston, M., Walmesley, B. and Ryan, J. (2008) 'Saying hello each day: Combating loneliness and isolation in Wigan Borough', project funded by National Lottery Community Fund, draft report and personal correspondence with authors.

Sheldon, J.H. (1948) *The social medicine of old age*, Oxford: Oxford University Press.

Silverstein, M. and Marenco, A. (2001) 'How Americans enact the granparent role across the family life course', *Journal of Family Issues*, 22, pp 493–522.

Smart, C., Neale, B. and Wade, A. (2001) *The changing experience of childhood: Families and divorce*, Cambridge: Polity.

Soule, A., Babb, P., Evandrou, M., Balchin, S. and Zealey, L. (2005) *Focus on older people, 2005 edn*, Office of National Statistics/Department for Work and Pensions, Basingstoke: Palgrave Macmillan.

Spencer, L. and Pahl, R. (2006) *Rethinking friendship: Hidden solidarities today*, Princeton, NJ: Princeton University Press.

Stearns, P. (1977) *Old age in European society*, London: Croom Helm.

Stone, L. (1977) *The family, sex and marriage in England, 1500–1800*, London: Weidenfeld and Nicolson.

Summerfield, P. (1989) *Women workers in the Second World War: Production and patriarchy in conflict*, London: Routledge.

Szinovacz, M. (1991) 'Women and retirement', in B. Hess and E. Markson (eds), *Growing old in America*, New York: Transaction, pp 293–303.

Szinovacz, M. (1998) *Handbook on grandparenthood*, Westport, CN: Greenwood Press.

Szinovacz, M. (2000) 'Changes in housework after retirement: A panel analysis', *Journal of Marriage and the Family*, 62, pp 78–92.

Szinovacz, M. and Schaffer, A. (2000) 'Effects of retirement on marital conflict management', *Journal of Family Issues*, 21, pp 367–89.

Thane, P. (2000) *Old age in English history*, Oxford: Oxford University Press.

Thompson, P. and Bauer, E. (2000) 'Jamaican transnational families: Points of pain and sources of resilience', *Wadabagei: A Journal of the Caribbean and its Diaspora*, 3, pp 1–37.

Thomson, D. (1986) 'Welfare and the historians', in L. Bonfield, R.M. Smith and K. Wrighton (eds), *The world we have gained: Histories of population and social structure*, Oxford: Basil Blackwell, pp 355–78.

Thomson, D. (1991) 'The welfare of the elderly in the past: A family or community responsibility?', in M. Pelling and R. Smith (eds), *Life, death and the elderly*, London: Routledge, pp 194–221.

Torres, S. (2006) 'Culture, migration, inequality, and "periphery" in a globalized world: Challenges for ethno- and anthropogerontology', in J. Baars, D. Dannefer, C. Phillipson and A. Walker (eds), *Aging, globalization and inequality: The new critical gerontology*, Amityville: Baywood Publishing Company, pp 231–44.

Townsend, P. (1957) *The family life of old people*, London: Routledge.

Twigg, J. and Atkin, K. (1994) *Carers perceived: Policy and practice in informal care*, Buckingham: Open University Press.

Van Den Hoonard, D.K. (2001) *The widowed self: Older women's journey through widowhood*, Ontario: Laurier University Press.

Van Den Hoonard, D.K. (2004) 'Attitudes of older widows and widowers in New Brunswick, Canada towards new partnerships', in K. Davidson and G. Fennell (eds), *Intimacy in later life*, New Brunswick, NJ: Transaction Publishers, pp 105–20.

Vertovec, S. (2001) *Transnational social formations: Towards conceptual cross-fertilization*, Center for Migration and Development Working Paper, Princeton, NJ: Princeton University Press.

Victor, C., Scrambler, S., Bond, J. and Bowling, A. (2004) 'Loneliness in later life: Preliminary findings from the Growing Older Project', in A. Walker and C. Hennessey (eds), *Quality of life in old age*, Maidenhead: Open University Press, pp 107–26.

Victor, C., Scrambler, S., Shah, S., Cook, D., Harris, T., Rink, E. and De Wilde, S. (2002) 'Has loneliness among older people increased? An investigation into variation between cohorts', *Ageing and Society*, 22, pp 1–13.

Von Volkholm, M. (2006) 'Sibling relationships in middle and older adulthood: A review of the literature', *Marriage and Family Review*, 40, pp 151–70.

Vullnetari, J. and King, R. (2008) '"Does your granny eat grass?" On mass migration, care drain and the fate of older people in rural Albania', *Global Networks*, 8, pp 139–71.

Walker, A., Allen, K. and Connidis, I. (2005) 'Methodological challenges: Theorizing and studying sibling ties in adulthood', in V.L. Bengtson, A. Acock, K. Allen, P. Dilworth-Anderson and D. Klein (eds), *Sourcebook of family theory and research*, Thousand Oaks, CA: Sage, Part 7, pp 167–90.

Walker R. and Luszcz, M. (2009) 'The health and relationship dynamics of late-life couples: A systematic review of the literature', *Ageing and Society*, 29, pp 455–80.

Wall, R. (1984) 'Residential isolation of the elderly over time: A comparison over time', *Ageing in Society*, 4, pp 483–503.

Wall, R. (1998) 'Intergenerational relationships past and present', in A. Walker (ed), *The new generational contract: Intergenerational relationships, old age and welfare*, London: UCL Press, pp 37–55.

Warnes, A., Freidrich, K., Kellaher, L. and Torres, S. (2004) 'The diversity and welfare of older migrants in Europe', *Ageing and Society*, 24, pp 307–26.

Weeks, J., Heaphy, B. and Donovan, C. (1999) 'Partnership rites: Commitment and ritual in non-heterosexual relationships', in J. Seymour and P. Bagguley (eds), *Relating intimacies: Power and resistance*, Basingstoke: Macmillan, pp 43–64.

Weston, K. (1991) *Families we choose: Lesbians, gays, kinship*, New York: Columbia University Press.

White. L. (2001) 'Sibling relationships over the life course: A panel analysis', *Journal of Marriage and the Family*, 63, pp 555-68.

White, L. and Riedmann, A. (1992) 'Ties among adult siblings', *Social Forces*, 71, pp 85–102.

Wilding, R. (2006) '"Virtual" intimacies? Families communicating across transnational contexts', *Global Networks*, 6, pp 125–42.

Willmott, P. and Young, M. (1960) *Family and class in a London suburb*, London: Routledge and Kegan Paul.

Winkelmann-Gleed, A. and Seely, J. (2005) 'Strangers in a British world? Integration of international nurses', *British Journal of Nursing*, 14, pp 954–61.

Young, M. and Willmott, P. (1957) *Family and kinship in East London*, London: Routledge and Kegan Paul.

Index